MATHEMATICAL DRAWING

BY

G. M. MINCHIN, M.A., F.R.S.

PROFESSOR OF APPLIED MATHEMATICS AT THE ROYAL INDIAN ENGINEERING COLLEGE,
COOPER'S HILL,

AND

J. B. DALE, M.A.

ASSISTANT PROFESSOR OF MATHEMATICS AT KING'S COLLEGE, LONDON.

SECOND EDITION

LONDON
EDWARD ARNOLD
41 & 43, MADDOX STREET, BOND STREET, W.

1909

PREFACE.

IN every branch of Mathematics we are presented with solutions of problems expressed in the form of equations from which some unknown quantity is to be found; and in many cases the mathematician is content to regard the equation as the complete solution of the problem without obtaining from it the actual value of the quantity sought. If, however, the problem is a physical one, we cannot be content to leave the unknown quantity buried in an equation. Sometimes the equation is one which falls under well-known algebraic rules and admits of a solution by standard methods; but in most cases, of course, physical equations do not assume the forms discussed in treatises on Algebra and Theory of Equations.

A considerable portion of this work is devoted to the discussion of such equations and the means by which they can be solved graphically.

An exposition of the methods to be employed in a large number of somewhat typical cases will assist the student to invent graphic methods for himself when he meets some equation which does not come precisely under any of the forms here discussed. A little practice is all that is necessary, and it is hoped that the examples contained in this book will prove to be an adequate guide.

This branch of our subject, although obviously of practical importance, is not very well known, or, so far as we are aware, systematically taught in schools or colleges.

The reader will, of course, bear in mind that, as the subject of the work is *Drawing*, a good deal of mathematical theory is assumed as within the knowledge of the student.

The second chapter is merely a collection of well-known constructions relating to the Conic Sections. The majority of them are to be found in the ordinary text-books of Geometrical Conics, and it is assumed that the reader is familiar with the leading theorems in this subject.

The last chapter deals with the construction of the projections of plane figures and especially with the projections of the circle. Not only is the method of projection one of great practical utility —it is used daily by the engineer, the builder, and the artist— but, from the point of view of pure mathematics, it introduces a unity into the development of the theory of the conic sections which is quite unattainable by the methods of 'Geometrical Conics.'

The fundamental principles are few and can be understood without difficulty by anyone possessing an elementary knowledge of Solid Geometry.

A connected account of the theory of the subject, so far as it is required for a comprehension of the constructions, has been given. But this account is nothing more than an outline; and for the higher developments and the theory of imaginary projection recourse must be had to the standard treatises on the subject.

G. M. M

J. B D.

September, 1906.

CONTENTS.

CHAPTER I.

ALGEBRAIC MULTIPLICATION, CIRCULAR ARCS, PLANIMETRIC MEASURES.

1. Graphic Multiplication. The product, $a \cdot b$, of two right lines, a and b, may be represented in two ways: it may be shown as the square of a line or as a unit length multiplied by a line.

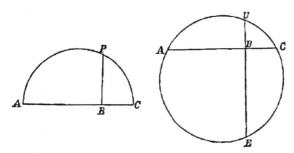

Fig. 1.

Let the two lines be AB and BC, Fig. 1, placed so that one is a continuation of the other. On AC as diameter describe a semicircle, and let a perpendicular at B to AC meet the circumference in P; then by Euclid III 8,

$$AB \times BC = BP^2.$$

·Or again, at B draw BU equal to unity, either perpendicular to AC or in any other direction, and describe a circle through the points A, U, C. If UB produced meets the circle in E, we have, by Euclid III 35,

$$AB \times BC = UB \times BE = BE,$$

since UB is a unit length.

2. Graphic Division. It is required to represent

$$\frac{a}{b}, \quad \frac{a^2}{b^2}, \quad \frac{a^3}{b^3}, \quad \cdots$$

where a and b are two given lengths.

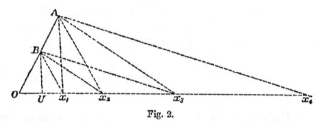

Fig. 2.

Let $OA = a$, $OB = b$ (Fig. 2), and draw OU equal to a unit length. Draw BU, and draw Ax_1 parallel to BU; draw Bx_1 and Ax_2 parallel to Bx_1; draw Bx_2 and Ax_3 parallel to it; and so on.

Then the lengths Ox_1, Ox_2, Ox_3,... represent $\frac{a}{b}$, $\left(\frac{a}{b}\right)^2$, $\left(\frac{a}{b}\right)^3$,....

For $\frac{Ox_1}{OU} = \frac{AO}{OB}$, $\therefore Ox_1 = \frac{a}{b}$; and similarly for the others.

These ratios can also be represented easily if OA and OB are along different lines; thus: take OU along OB equal to a unit; from U draw Ux_1 parallel to AB meeting OA in x_1; let an arc of radius Ox_1 cut OB in y_1; from y_1 draw y_1x_2 parallel to AB meeting OA in x_2; let an arc of radius Ox_2 cut OB in y_2; from y_2 draw y_2x_3 parallel to AB; and so on. Then the lengths Ox_1, Ox_2, Ox_3,... represent the successive powers of the ratio $\frac{a}{b}$.

We have frequently to represent $\sin^2\theta$, $\sin^3\theta$, &c., and of course this can be done by taking $OA = 1$, $OB = \sin\theta$, $OU = OA = 1$ and proceeding as above, the ratio now being $\frac{OB}{OA}$; we draw AU and Bx_1 parallel to it; then Ax_1 and Bx_2 parallel to it; and so on.

The successive multiplications by $\sin\theta$, $\sin^2\theta$,... can be shown also thus: let $AB = a$ (Fig. 3), and $CBA = \theta$; if AC is drawn perpendicular to BC, CP to AB, PQ to AC, QR to AB, and so on, we have $AC = a\sin\theta$, $AP = a\sin^2\theta$, $AQ = a\sin^3\theta$, $AR = a\sin^4\theta$.

In the same way multiplications by successive powers of $\cos \theta$, $\tan \theta$, and other trigonometrical ratios can be represented.

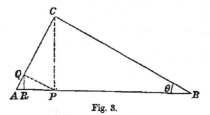

Fig. 3.

3. The Diagonal Scale. Let OA and OB (Fig. 4) be two right lines each of length a including any angle (in the figure a

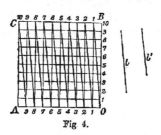

Fig 4.

right angle); let each of them be divided into ten equal parts; join O to the end of the first division of BC; join the end of the first division of OA to the end of the second of BC, and so on, as represented in the figure. Then the length of the intercept made by the line $O1$, which joins O to the end of the first division of BC, on a line parallel to OA drawn through the 6th division of OB, counted from O is $\cdot 06 \times a$; and if the line parallel to OA is drawn through the nth division of OB counted from O, the intercept is

$$\cdot 0n \times a.$$

The length of the line between the division 3 of OB and the line 78 which joins the 7th division of OA to the 8th of BC is clearly

$$\cdot 03 \times a + \cdot 7 \times a, \; i.e., \; \cdot 73 \times a.$$

Hence the number along OA indicates the first decimal place and that along OB the second in measuring this length.

To find to two decimal places the length of the line l', we open the dividers to the length of l' and then slide the end of one of the legs along OB and, keeping the line joining the points of the legs parallel to OA, find the sloping line on which the point of the second leg rests. We find that when the point of one leg is at 4 on OB, the point of the other rests on the sloping line through 5 on OA; hence

$$l' = \cdot 54 \times a.$$

Similarly we find $l = \cdot 73 \times a.$

We can, of course, vary the diagonal scale by making OA and OB of different lengths and dividing each of them into the same number of equal parts, whether 10 or any other.

4. Graphic representation of π. The following extremely accurate representation of the length of the circumference of a circle dates from the year 1685 and is due to a Pole named Kochansky.

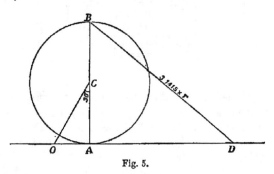

Fig. 5.

Let AB (Fig. 5) be a diameter of the circle and C the centre; at A draw the tangent; draw CO making the angle $ACO = 30°$; from O measure $OD = 3r$, where $r =$ radius of circle; then

$$BD = 3\cdot 1415 \times r,$$

and therefore BD is a very close approximation to the length of the semi-circumference.

5. Length of any circular arc. To represent the length of any circular arc less than a quadrant, the following method can be adopted. Let AP, Fig. 6, be the arc; produce its chord

PA to P' so that $AP' = \frac{1}{2}AP$; with P' as centre and radius $P'P$ describe a circular arc cutting the tangent AE in Q; then

$$\text{arc } AP = \text{length } AQ.$$

This is true to a high order of approximation; for, if θ is the circular measure of the angle ACP subtended by the arc AP at the centre C, we can show that

$$AQ = r\theta \left(1 - \frac{\theta^4}{1080} - \text{higher terms in } \theta\right).$$

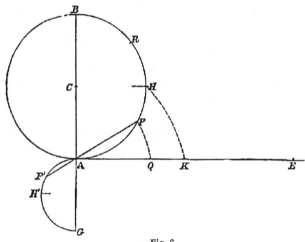

Fig. 6.

Hence AQ is very slightly less than the length of the arc AP, the defect being (if we neglect the small terms beyond θ^4) the fraction $\dfrac{\theta^4}{1080}$ of the length of the arc.

Even for a quadrant, this fraction is only ·0056371, or about the $\frac{1}{180}$th part of the whole arc. We may therefore regard the approximation as quite satisfactory even for a quadrant.

For arcs greater than a quadrant, this method combined with the result of Art. 4, gives the lengths with the same accuracy.

If we produce the diameter BA to G so that $AG =$ the radius, and on AG as diameter describe a circle, any chord, PA, meets this circle in a point P' such that $AP' = \frac{1}{2}AP$. Let AH be a quadrant, and let HA meet this circle in H'. If the circle with

centre H' and radius $H'H$ meets AE in K, then AK is the length
of the quadrant; and if we lay off $AE =$ the semi-circle AHB,
by using the method of Art. 4, we see that AK measures exactly
$\frac{1}{2}AE$.

For an arc AHR greater than a quadrant, we simply lay off
from A an arc equal to the arc BR, and find the length of
BR; and the difference between this and AE is the length of the
arc AHR.

6. Theory of Amsler's Planimeter. If a right line, 11′,
Fig. 7, is displaced in any manner in a plane, it has at each
instant during its motion an instantaneous centre, I, about which
it is performing a pure rotation. This is the fundamental theorem
of the uniplanar kinematics of a rigid body. The position of I
is found by drawing perpendiculars at 1 and 1′ to the directions of
motion of these points. The foot, i, of the perpendicular from
I on the line is the point in which the line intersects its next
consecutive position, 22′, *i.e.*, the point of contact of the line with
its envelope.

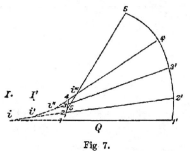

Fig 7.

The area enclosed by the two curves along which the ends
1 and 1′ of the line are displaced and any two positions—say
11′ and 55′—of the line is the *algebraic* sum of the infinitesimal
elements of area traced out by the successive infinitely close
positions of the line. In the figure the end 1 after moving
forward to 2, 3, and 4, moves backwards to 5; and it is clear that
in order that the area inside the circuit 11′2′3′4′5′51 should be
the sum of the area inside the circuit 11′2′3′4′41 and the area
determined by the crossed lines 44′ and 55′, the area $i'''45$ must
be taken negatively. But this is quite in accordance with mathe-

matical calculation, and comes under the rule that *in estimating the area of any closed circuit we imagine ourselves travelling continuously round it in a given sense, and we take as positive all the area at the left-hand side and as negative every part at the right.* Thus, then, the algebraic value of the crossed area $4'5'544'$ is area $4'i'''5' -$ area $4i'''5$.

To express the element of area $11'2'2$ traced out by the line in moving from a first position $11'$ into the consecutive position $22'$, let the motion be produced by two successive operations—

    $1°$. Let the end 1 be fixed and the line $11'$ rotated through an angle $d\phi$ until it is parallel to $22'$;

    $2°$. Let the line now be moved perpendicular to itself through a distance dR until it coincides with $22'$.

If l is the length of the line, the element of area, dA, is given by the expression

$$dA = \tfrac{1}{2}l^2 d\phi + l\,dR, \quad\quad\quad\quad\quad (1)$$

the term $\tfrac{1}{2}l^2 d\phi$ being the area of the little triangle described in motion $1°$, and the term $l\,.\,dR$ the area of the little parallelogram described in the motion $2°$.

This agrees with what has been said of the crossed area $4'5'54$, because if we rotate the line $44'$ about 4 until it is parallel to $55'$ the rotation $d\phi$ is counterclockwise, and the subsequent rolling is in the opposite sense, so that for this figure dR is negative, and the element of area $= 4'5'i''' - 45i'''$, as before.

The whole area from any first to any final position is given therefore by

$$A = \tfrac{1}{2}l^2 \int d\phi + l \int dR. \quad\quad\quad\quad (2)$$

Here $\int d\phi$ is the whole angle through which the line has revolved from the first position, and $\int dR$ is the sum of the motions of the point 1 perpendicular to the instantaneous positions of the moving line. If the end $1'$ is carried round a closed curve and brought back to its original place, while the end 1 is carried over a portion of an unclosed curve and brought back to its first position so that the line has not rotated on the whole, A is the area of the closed curve itself, and $\int d\phi = 0$; so that

$$A = l \, . \int dR. \quad \dots\dots\dots\dots\dots\dots\dots(3)$$

This is the result in the most usual employment of Amsler's planimeter; but sometimes the line is brought back to its original position by having been allowed to rotate through 2π; and if this is so, the area of the closed curve is given by

$$A = \pi l^2 + l \int dR. \quad \dots\dots\dots\dots\dots\dots (4)$$

In any position, 11', of the line the displacement of any point, Q, on it is easily found; for, Q moves perpendicular to IQ, and its displacement is $IQ \, . \, d\phi$ when the line rotates through $d\phi$. The component of this displacement perpendicular to the line is $IQ d\phi \times \cos IQi$, *i.e.*,

$$\text{motion of } Q \text{ perp. to line} = iQ \, . \, d\phi \quad \dots\dots\dots\dots(5)$$

Let us suppose the moving line to be a bar with a tracing pin fixed to it at the end 1'. The integral motion of any point Q on the bar perpendicular to the bar is obtained by fixing a small graduated roller to the bar at Q, the axis of the roller lying accurately in the line of the tracing points 11'. If the roller were fixed at Q, the element of area 11'2'2, or dA, would be expressed as

$$l dR + \tfrac{1}{2} (a^2 - b^2) \, d\phi, \quad \dots\dots\dots\dots\dots\dots (6)$$

where $a = Q1'$ and $b = Q1$, and dR is the motion registered by the roller. If the roller is fixed at 1', and dR' is its reading,

$$dA = l dR' - \tfrac{1}{2} l^2 d\phi. \quad \dots\dots\dots\dots\dots\dots(7)$$

The roller is invariably fixed near 1 because it is more easily protected from accident in that position.

It is not necessary to know the length l between the points 1 and 1', and in some forms of the Amsler planimeter the point 1' can be drawn out through a considerable distance from 1, one part of the arm consisting of a tube sliding over the other. When we do not know l, we measure some known simple area such as a square of 2 inches side. If then we use the instrument in such a way that $\int d\phi = 0$, and if r is the whole reading of the roller when the known square is traversed by the tracing point 1', we have

$$l \cdot r = a^2 = \text{known square},$$

and if R is the whole reading of the roller when any other closed curve, of area A, is traversed,

$$lR = A,$$

$$\therefore \quad A = \frac{R}{r} a^2,$$

which eliminates l.

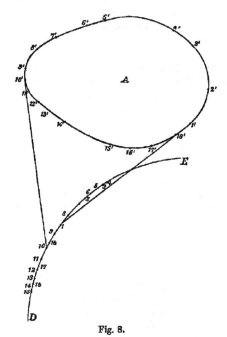

Fig. 8.

Fig. 8 represents the various simultaneous positions of the ends 1, 1', &c. of an arm of constant length, one end travelling from the position 1' round a closed curve, A, while the other merely oscillates between the extreme points of a limited arc DE.

The simultaneous points 1, 1'; 2, 2', &c. are given in order that the student may follow out the various elements of area typified in Fig. 7 and satisfy himself that positive and negative portions outside the area A cancel each other in the completed motion, according to the principles explained above.

Nothing depends on the nature of the curve DE: it may be a circle, as it is in Amsler's planimeter, because it is by far the most manageable curve; or it may be a right line, as, for example, in the crank and connecting rod system of a steam-engine. In this latter case we have a veritable planimeter in which the tracing point $1'$ is the crank pin, and the point 1 is the slide block. If a roller were fixed at this end perpendicularly to the connecting rod, the instrument would give us the area of the crank circle.

7. Centres of gravity and moments of inertia. By the measurement of areas with a planimeter we are enabled to find the position of the centre of gravity of any plane area, and also the moment of inertia of the area about any line in its plane.

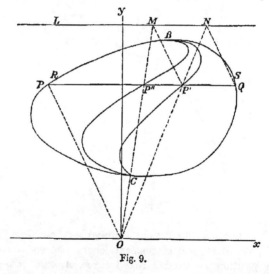

Fig. 9.

Let $BPCQB$, Fig. 9, be any curve bounding an area whose centre of gravity is to be found. Draw any line Ox in the plane, and draw LN parallel to Ox at any convenient distance, h. Divide the area into a large number of narrow strips parallel to Ox, of which $PQSR$ is the type. Let PQ be at a distance y from Ox, and RS at a distance dy from PQ. Then the area of the strip is $PQ.dy$, and its "mass moment" about Ox is

$$PQ.y.dy. \quad \dots \dots \dots \dots (1)$$

From Q draw QN parallel to OP, O being any point chosen on Ox; draw ON meeting PQ in P'; and by drawing a large number of lines parallel to Ox and repeating this process for all of them, find the curve, $BP'C$, which is the locus of P'.

Now, by similar triangles

$$\frac{PP'}{P'Q} = \frac{y}{h-y}, \quad \therefore PP' = \frac{y}{h}.PQ. \dots \dots \dots (2)$$

Hence the mass moment (1) is

$$h.PP'.dy. \quad \dots \dots \dots \dots (3)$$

As the mass moment of the whole area about Ox is the integral of (1), we see that this mass moment is

$$h \int PP'.dy,$$

that is $h \times$ area $BPCP'B$. Now the distance, $\bar{y}$, of the centre of gravity of the area $BCPQB$ from Ox is the mass moment divided by the area itself. If, then, we denote by A the given area and by A' the area $BPCP'B$, we have

$$\bar{y} = \frac{A'}{A}.h, \quad \dots \dots \dots \dots (4)$$

which gives $\bar{y}$ by the measurement of the areas A and A'.

Similarly the distance of the centre of gravity from any other line is found, and hence the position of the point.

Moment of inertia of given area about Ox. The moment of inertia of the typical strip $PQSR$ about Ox is $PQ.dy \times y^2$. Now from the curve $BP'C$ derive another, $BP''C$, by the same process as that by which $BP'C$ was derived from BPC; that is, from P' draw $P'M$ parallel to OP, and draw OM meeting PP' in P''; then

$$PP'' = \frac{y}{h}.PP' = \frac{y^2}{h^2}.PQ.$$

Hence $PQ . y^2 \, dy = h^2 . PP'' . dy$, so that the moment of inertia of the given area, which is $\int PQ . y^2 . dy$, is

$$h^2 . \int PP'' . dy \quad \text{or} \quad h^2 . A'',$$

where A'' is the area $BPCP''B$. If k is the radius of gyration about Ox, we have, then,

$$k^2 = \frac{A''}{A} . h^2. \qquad \qquad \dots \dots \dots \dots (5)$$

Since we can find also the moment of inertia about Oy, perpendicular to Ox, we have the polar moment of inertia about O from the fact that

$$k_3^2 = k_1^2 + k_2^2,$$

where k_1, k_2 are the radii of gyration about Ox and Oy, and k_3 the radius of gyration about the line at O perpendicular to the plane of the figure.

EXAMPLES.

1. Given two right lines OA and OB, and a point P between them, through P draw a right line meeting them in Q and R respectively, so that—

        (a) $QP = PR$,

        (b) $QP : PR = m : n$,

where m and n are given.

2. Given the centre of a conic and also any two tangents, find the direction of their chord of contact.

3. Inscribe in a given triangle another triangle the directions of whose sides are given.

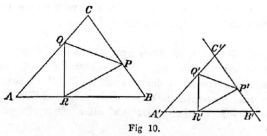

Fig 10.

Let ABC, Fig. 10, be the given triangle, and PQR the required triangle the directions of whose sides are given.

Describe any triangle, $P'Q'R'$, whose sides are in the given directions; through P' draw a line, $B'C'$, parallel to BC; through Q' a parallel, $A'C'$, to AC; and through R' a parallel, $A'B'$, to AB. We have thus a triangle $A'B'C'$ similar to ABC; and the second figure is similar to the first. Hence we have merely to divide BC at P similarly to $B'C'$ at P'; and so on.

4. By means of examples 2 and 3, construct a conic for which three tangents and the centre are given.

(By finding the chords of contact, we have a sufficient number of points from which to construct the conic by Maclaurin's method. See Chap. 4.)

5. Inscribe an equilateral triangle in a given triangle. How many solutions are there?

6. Inscribe a square in a given triangle, a side of the square lying along a side of the triangle.

Inscribe also a parallelogram similar to a given one.

7. If the area $BPCQB$ is a parallelogram or a triangle, draw the curves which determine the centre of gravity and the moment of inertia, choosing the most convenient positions of O and values of h.

8. Draw a semicircle, and verify by the planimeter that the centre of gravity of the area is $\frac{4}{3\pi} r$ from the centre, r being the radius. Verify also that the radius of gyration about the diameter is $\frac{1}{2}r$.

9. Take the area of a parabola cut off by any double ordinate, at distance h from the vertex, and verify by the planimeter that the centre of gravity is $\frac{2}{5}h$ from the vertex, and that the radius of gyration of the area about the tangent at the vertex is $h\left(\frac{3}{7}\right)^{\frac{1}{2}}$.

Many other well-known examples of centres of gravity and radii of gyration may be treated by the student with a planimeter.

CHAPTER II.

CONSTRUCTION OF CONICS BY METRICAL METHODS.

IN this chapter the principal methods of constructing conic sections in which measurements of length are involved, will be explained. Those methods of construction which depend upon the theory of projection will be found in the last chapter.

With a given set of data, the construction of the conic can generally be performed in more than one way, but as a general rule it will be found that projective methods of construction are preferable when the conic is required to pass through given points or touch given lines; while metrical methods are to be preferred when the focus, directrix, centre, conjugate diameters or axes are included in the data.

8. Given the focus, directrix and excentricity, to construct the conic.

First method, by means of the excentric circle.

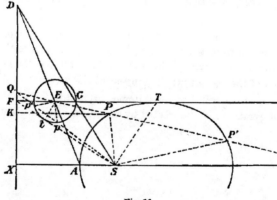

Fig. 11.

Let S be the focus, XD the directrix, e the excentricity. Then A the vertex divides SX in the ratio $e:1$.

Take any point E, and let AE meet the directrix at D. Join SD and let it cut EF drawn at right angles to the directrix in G. Then EG is the radius of the *excentric circle* whose centre is E, and $\dfrac{EG}{EF} = \dfrac{SA}{AX} = e$.

To obtain points on the curve, take any point Q on the directrix and draw QE and QS, the latter cutting the excentric circle at p and p'. From S draw SP, SP' parallel to Ep, Ep' respectively and meeting QE in P and P'. Then P and P' are points on the curve, for drawing PK perpendicular to the directrix,

$$\frac{SP}{Ep} = \frac{PQ}{EQ} = \frac{PK}{EF},$$

and therefore $\qquad \dfrac{SP}{PK} = \dfrac{Ep}{EF} = e.$

Similarly P' can be shown to be a point of the curve.

If St, St' be the tangents from S to the excentric circle meeting the directrix in $L*$ and L', then ST, ST' parallel to Et, Et' will meet Lt and Lt' respectively in the points of contact of the tangents from E to the curve.

Second method.

Let S be the focus, XD the directrix. At S erect SL at right angles to the axis SX, and take L so that $SL = eSX$. Then L is

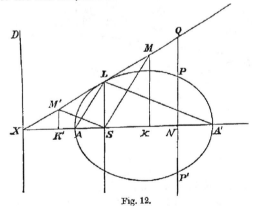

Fig. 12.

* In the figure L coincides with F.

one extremity of the latus rectum and a point on the curve The other extremity is at an equal distance from S on the other side of SX.

In SX take points K and K' such that $SK = SK' = SL$, and erect perpendiculars to SX at K to K' meeting XL in M and M'. Join SM and draw LA parallel to SM. Then A is a vertex. Join SM' and draw LA' parallel to SM', then A' is the other vertex. It is easily seen that A and A' are the vertices, for

$$\frac{SA}{AX} = \frac{LM}{XL} = \frac{SK}{SX} = \frac{SL}{SX} = e.$$

In the same manner we can prove that A' is also on the curve.

To obtain other points of the curve draw any number of lines at right angles to the axis. Let QN be one of these lines meeting the axis in N and XL in Q. With centre S and radius NQ describe a circle cutting NQ in P and P', then P and P' are points on the curve, because

$$\frac{SP}{NX} = \frac{SP'}{NX} = \frac{QN}{NX} = \frac{SL}{SX} = e.$$

9. **Given the focus and three points on a conic, to construct the curve.**

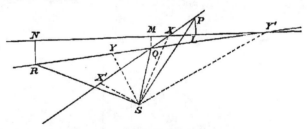

Fig 13.

Let S be the focus, P, Q, R the points. Join SP, SQ, SR and let the internal and external bisectors of the angle PSQ, QSR meet PQ and QR in the points X, X', Y, Y'. Then any one of the four lines XX', XY, XY', YY', is the directrix of a conic whose focus is S and which passes through the three given points.

Take for example the line XY' and draw perpendiculars PL, QM, RN to this line. Then

$$\frac{SP}{SQ} = \frac{PX}{QX} = \frac{PL}{QM} \text{ and } \frac{SQ}{SR} = \frac{QY'}{RY'} = \frac{QM}{RN},$$

and therefore $$\frac{SP}{PL} = \frac{SQ}{QM} = \frac{SR}{RN}.$$

EXAMPLES.

1. Given the directrix and three points, construct the conic.

2. Given the focus, two points and a tangent at one of the points, construct the conic.

3. Given the directrix, two points and a tangent at one of the points, construct the conic.

4. Given two points, the focus and the excentricity, construct the conic.

5. Given two points, the directrix and the excentricity, construct the conic.

10. Given the axis, the vertex and another point on a parabola, to construct the curve.

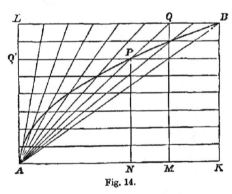

Fig. 14.

Let A be the vertex, AK the axis, and B another point. Let BK be the perpendicular drawn from B to the axis. Complete the rectangle $BKAL$.

Divide AL and LB into any, the same number of equal parts, and through the points of division of AL draw lines parallel to

M. D. 2

the axis. Let Q be one of the points of division of LB, and Q' the corresponding point on AL so that $\dfrac{LQ}{LB} = \dfrac{AQ'}{AL}$. Then if AQ cuts the line through Q' in P, P is a point on the parabola.

Draw QM and PN perpendicular to the axis.

Then
$$\frac{PN}{QM} = \frac{AN}{AM} = \frac{AN}{LQ},$$

and
$$\frac{PN}{QM} = \frac{AQ'}{AL} = \frac{LQ}{LB}.$$

Hence $\dfrac{PN^2}{QM^2} = \dfrac{AN}{LB}$ or $PN^2 = \dfrac{QM^2}{LB} AN = \dfrac{BK^2}{AK} AN.$

Therefore P is a point on a parabola, whose latus rectum is equal to $\dfrac{BK^2}{AK}$.

11. Given the focus of a parabola and the tangent at the vertex, to construct the curve.

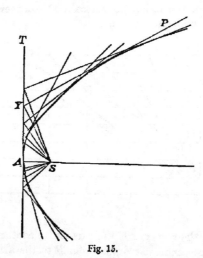

Fig. 15.

Let S be the focus, and AT the tangent at the vertex, A being the foot of the perpendicular from S upon the tangent. Then A is the vertex.

From S draw any line ST meeting the tangent at the vertex in Y, and through Y draw YP at right angles to SY. YP will be a tangent to the parabola, and by taking different positions of Y, any number of tangents can be drawn and the curve constructed as the envelope of these lines.

12. Given three points on a parabola and the direction of the axis, to determine the focus and to construct the curve.

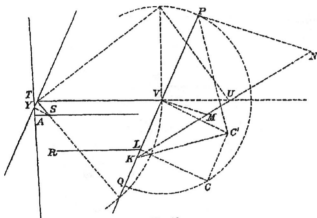

Fig. 16.

Let PQR be the three points. Join PQ, and draw RL parallel to the axis meeting PQ in L. Bisect PQ at V and through V draw TV parallel to the axis. We have first to determine T, the point in which this line cuts the parabola.

Since TV is parallel to RL we have

$$\frac{TV}{RL} = \frac{PV^2}{PL.LQ} = \frac{PV^2}{LC^2} = \frac{PV}{VK} = \frac{NM}{MK} = \frac{NM}{RL}*.$$

This determines the length of TV.

If L lies between P and Q, then T must be taken upon the same side of PQ as R; but if L does not lie between P and Q then T must be taken upon the opposite side of PQ to R.

T is the vertex of the diameter bisecting PQ, and if S is the focus

$$PV^2 = TV.VU = 4ST.TV.$$

* The construction is indicated in the figure. See Chap. ɪ § 1.

Also ST and TV are equally inclined to the tangent at T, or to the chord PQ, and therefore the position of S is determined.

From S draw SY at right angles to the tangent at T meeting it at Y, and through Y draw YA so that the angle STY is equal to the angle SYA.

Then YA is the tangent at the vertex, and the curve can be constructed.

13. Given four points on a parabola, to construct the curve.

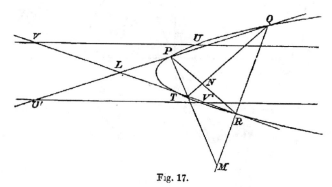

Fig. 17.

Let $PQRT$ be the four points, and let PQ, RT intersect in L; QR, PT in M and QT, PR in N. Then the tangents drawn from L to the parabola will meet the curve upon KM (Chap. IV § 102).

Upon PQ take two points U, U' such that
$$LU^2 = LU'^2 = LP \cdot LQ.$$
and upon RT take two points V, V', such that
$$LV^2 = LV'^2 = LR \ LT.$$

Then UV and $U'V'$ are diameters of a parabola through the four points, and UV', $U'V$ are diameters of a second parabola through the four points.

These diameters will meet NM in the points of contact of the tangents drawn from L.

The direction of the axis now being known, the construction of the curve may be carried out as in the preceding case.

EXAMPLES.

1. Given a diameter of a parabola, the tangent at its extremity, and a point on the curve, construct the parabola.

2. Given the focus, a tangent and its point of contact, construct the parabola.

3. Construct a parabola, given the focus and two points on the curve.

4. Construct a parabola, given the focus and two tangents to the curve.

5. Construct a parabola, given the focus, the direction of the axis and a tangent.

6. Construct a parabola, given the direction of the axis, two points on the curve and the tangent at one of them.

7. Given a parabola determine its axis and focus.

14. Given the axes of an ellipse, to construct the curve.

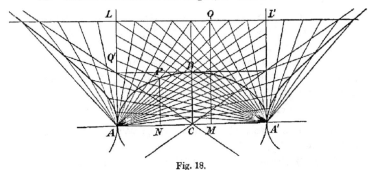

Fig. 18.

Let AA' be the transverse axis, CB the semi-minor axis. Upon AA' describe the rectangle $ALL'A'$, having the side AL equal to the minor axis.

Divide AL and LL' into any, the same number of equal parts. Let Q be a point of division of LL' and Q' the corresponding point of division of AL such that

$$\frac{AQ'}{AL} = \frac{LQ}{LL'} \quad \text{or} \quad \frac{AQ'}{BC} = \frac{LQ}{AC}.$$

Join AQ, $A'Q'$, then P the point of intersection of these lines is a point on the ellipse.

Draw QM and PN perpendicular to AA', then

$$\frac{PN}{NA'} = \frac{AQ'}{AA'} \quad \text{and} \quad \frac{PN}{AN} = \frac{QM}{AM}.$$

Hence

$$\frac{PN^2}{AN.NA'} = \frac{AQ'}{2AC} \cdot \frac{2BC}{LQ} = \frac{BC^2}{AC^2},$$

and therefore P is a point on the ellipse whose axes are AA' and $2CB$.

When a quarter of the curve has been so constructed, the remainder is easily obtained by reason of the symmetry about the axes.

A *hyperbola* with the same axes may be constructed by measuring either AQ' or LQ in the directions opposite to those in which they are measured in the construction of the ellipse. It is easily seen that the asymptotes are the lines through C parallel to AL' and $A'L$.

15. Given the transverse axis and the foci of an ellipse, to construct the curve.

Let AA' be the transverse axis, S and S' the foci. Upon AA' as diameter describe a circle. Take any point P upon the circumference, join SP and through P draw a line PT at right angles to SP. PT will be a tangent to the ellipse, and by taking different positions for P, the curve may be constructed as the envelope of a set of tangents.

The same construction may be used for the *hyperbola*.

16. Given two foci and a point on an ellipse, to construct the curve.

Since the sum of the focal distances of any point upon an ellipse is equal to the transverse axis, the length of the transverse axis can be at once found, and the curve constructed in the manner shown in the preceding article.

Otherwise, with S and S' as centres describe any number of pairs of circles such that the sum of the radii of corresponding circles is equal to the sum of the focal distances of the given point. Then the points of intersection of corresponding circles will be points on the ellipse.

An exactly similar construction, using differences instead of sums of focal distances, will give points upon a hyperbola. (See also Chap. III §§ 28, 29.)

17. Given a tangent to an ellipse or a hyperbola and the two foci, to construct the curve.

Let SS' be the foci, LM the tangent. From S draw SY at right angles to LM and produce it to T, so that $SY = YT$. Join $S'T$ and let it meet LM in P. Then P is the point of contact of the tangent. A point on the curve and two foci are now known and the curve may be constructed as before.

18. Given a pair of conjugate diameters, to construct the principal axes of the ellipse.

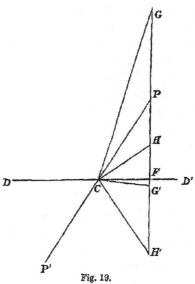

Fig. 19.

When a pair of conjugate diameters are given the conic may be constructed by the method of Article 14, taking $ALL'A'$ as a parallelogram with its sides parallel to the given diameters.

Let PCP', DCD' be the conjugate diameters.

From P draw PF perpendicular to CD, and upon it take G and G' so that $PG = PG' = CD$. Join CG, CG' and let CH, CH', the internal and external bisectors of the angle GCG', meet PF in H and H'. Then CH, CH' are the axes of the ellipse and the lengths of the axes are equal to the sum and difference respectively of CG and CG'.

The transverse axis is that which lies in the acute angle between the diameters.

19. Given the centre and three points on an ellipse, to construct the curve.

Let C be the centre, P, Q, R the three points. Join PQ, bisect it at M, then CM is the direction of the diameter conjugate to PQ.

Through C draw a line CL parallel to PQ, this will be the direction of the diameter conjugate to CM.

Draw RLR' parallel to CM, meeting CL at L, and such that $RL = LR'$. Then R' will be a point on the curve.

If E be the point of intersection of PQ and RR', and CA, CB the lengths of the diameters in the directions CM and CL

$$EQ \cdot EP : ER \cdot ER' = CB^2 : CA^2.$$

Also if RN parallel to CB meets CA in N,

$$EQ \cdot EP : ER \cdot ER' = RN^2 : CA^2 - CN^2.$$

To determine CA and CB, describe any two circles through PQ and RR', and let EK and ET be the tangents drawn from E to each of them.

Construct X, a fourth proportional to EK, ET and RN, so that

$$EK^2 : ET^2 = RN^2 : X^2$$

or $$EQ \cdot EP : ER \cdot ER' = RN^2 : X^2.$$

Hence $CA^2 = CN^2 + X^2$ and is found as the hypotenuse of a right-angled triangle whose sides are CN and X.

CB may then be found, since

$$CB : CA = EK : ET.$$

Two conjugate diameters are thus found and the ellipse can be constructed.

20. Given the asymptotes of a hyperbola and a tangent, to construct the curve.

Let CF, CF' be the asymptotes, PQ the tangent meeting the asymptotes in P and Q' respectively.

Upon CF on the side of C remote from P take P' so that $CP' = CQ$. Describe a circle passing through the points P and P'. Through C draw any number of chords such as $L'CM'$. Then if points L and M be taken upon CF and CF' so that $CL = CL'$ and $CM = CM'$ then LM will be a tangent to the curve. For

$$CL \cdot CM = CL' \cdot CM' = CP \cdot CP' = CP \cdot CQ,$$

and therefore the variable line LM forms a triangle of constant area with the two lines CF and CF'. Hence it envelopes a hyperbola.

EXAMPLES.

1.   Construct an ellipse, given a focus and three tangents.

2.   Construct an ellipse, given a focus, two tangents and the point of contact of one of them.

3.   Construct an ellipse, given a focus, two points and the tangent at one of the points.

4.   Construct an ellipse, passing through five given points.

5.   Construct an ellipse, given a focus, the length of the major axis a point on the curve and a tangent.

6.   Construct a hyperbola, having given the asymptotes and a point on the curve.

7.   Construct a hyperbola, given the asymptotes and a focus.

8.   Construct a hyperbola, given one asymptote, a focus and a point on the curve.

9.   Construct a hyperbola, given one asymptote, a directrix and a point on the curve.

CHAPTER III.

VARIOUS CURVES.

GRAPHIC SOLUTION OF EQUATIONS

21. To draw the Cycloid. Let $AP'B$ be a circle, and as in Art. 5, draw on AG as diameter a circle of half the radius. Let $AE =$ the semicircle $AP'R'B$; let $P'A$ meet the small circle in P''; with P'' as centre and radius $P''P'$ describe an arc cutting

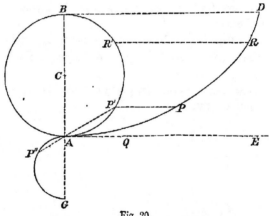

Fig. 20.

AE in Q; then $AQ =$ arc AP'; draw $P'P$ equal and parallel to AQ; then P is a point on the cycloid, draw $P'R'$ parallel to AB; then arc $AR' = QE$; from R' draw $R'R$ equal and parallel to QE; then R is on the cycloid.

Drawing any other chords such as $P'AP''$, we obtain as many points as we please on the cycloid. Only one-half of the curve is shown, viz., $APRD$; there is another to the left of AB.

Among the simple properties of the cycloid may be mentioned·

(a) the tangent at P is parallel to the chord AP';

(b) the length of the arc $AP = 2 \times$ length of chord AP' Hence the whole length of the cycloid is four times the diameter, AB, of the generating circle;

(c) the area of the whole cycloid is three times the area of the generating circle.

22. The Curve of Sines. To construct the curve $y = \sin x$, where x is, of course, a circular measure. Draw a circle with centre C (Fig. 21) and radius CA equal to a unit length; on the production of the line CA take any point O from which on the line OD the values of x are measured.

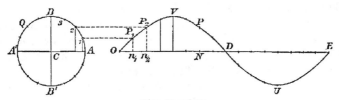

Figs. 21 and 22.

If x is the length of any arc of the circle measured from A, we must have the means of representing x along OD measured from O To effect this, measure OD (Fig. 22) equal to the semi-circumference of the circle, $i e$, $OD = \pi r$. Here π may be taken as $\frac{22}{7}$, and as r is a unit, $OD = 3\frac{1}{7}$ units. Or we may lay off the semi-circumference by the method of Art. 4.

Now divide the semi-circumference into any number of equal parts at the points 1, 2, 3, ..., and divide OD into the *same* number of equal parts at the points n_1, n_2, n_3, ...

Any arc, such as $A2$, on the circle is now equal to a known length, On_2, along OD; and an arc AQ is equal to a known length ON along OD.

Now consider the angle $AC1$. Its sine is the perpendicular from 1 on CA; so that if from the point 1 we draw an indefinite line $1P_1$ parallel to CAO, and at n_1 draw a perpendicular n_1P_1 to OD to meet this line, we see that the ordinate P_1n_1 is the sine

Hence, then, from the points 1, 2, 3, ... of the circle draw parallels to the axis $CAOD$, and at the corresponding points n_1, n_2, n_3, ... erect perpendiculars and we obtain points P_1, P_2, P_3, ... on the required curve of sines, since the ordinates $P_1 n_1$, $P_2 n_2$, $P_3 n_3$, ... are the sines of the corresponding values, On_1, On_2, On_3, ... of x.

The curve will cut the axis ODE at the point D, since the sine of the angle subtended at C by the arc AA' is zero; and the ordinates will be reproduced at the lower side of ODE, the ordinate vanishing at E, where $OE = 2OD =$ whole circumference of circle.

Beyond E the curve will exactly repeat itself; and OE is called the *wave-length* of the curve. It is, of course, obvious that the curve can be drawn by method of Art. 5.

If for the drawing of the curve of sines we adopt the method of measuring circular arcs given in Art. 5, the process will be as follows: let OA, Fig. 23, be a quadrant, OQ the tangent at O, and OB at right angles to OQ. Take OD equal to the radius of the circle, and on OD as diameter describe a semi-circle. Let $P'OP''$

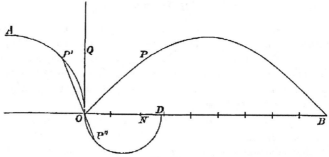

Fig 23.

be any line through O; with P'' as centre and $P''P'$ as radius draw a circular arc cutting OQ in Q, measure ON equal to OQ, and at N draw an ordinate NP to meet the line through P' parallel to OB; then P is on the curve of sines.

OB, a semi-circumference of the circle, may be marked in degrees. Thus in the figure if we mark 180° at B, the ends of the nine equal divisions along OB would be marked 20°, 40°, 60°, ... 180°.

Let us take the curve as given by an equation of less restricted form, and for clearness let us take numerical coefficients. Thus, let it be required to construct the curve

$$y = 7 \sin \frac{x-5}{4}.$$

We see now that the radius of the circle $ABA'B'$ must be taken equal to 4, and that another circle, of radius 7, will be required, so that the construction is as follows:

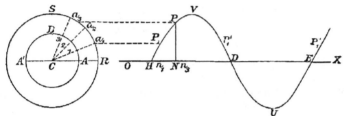

Figs. 24 and 25.

Describe a circle ABA' (Fig. 24) of radius 4 units, and with the same centre another, RS, with radius 7 units; if O is the origin from which the length x is measured along the axis, OX, of x (Fig. 25), measure OH equal to 5 units in the positive direction of the axis, and from H measure HD equal to the length of the semi-circumference of the circle ABA'; divide the arc ABA', as before, into any number of equal parts, and divide HD into the same; produce the radii $C1, C2, C3, \ldots$ to cut the circle RS in $a_1, a_2, a_3, \ldots$; from these points draw parallels to COX to meet the ordinates drawn at $n_1, n_2, n_3, \ldots$ and the points of intersection determine the required curve. For, suppose that we take the point n_1; then On_1 is its x, $\therefore Hn_1$ is $x-5$, and the circular measure of the angle RCa_1 is $\frac{A1}{CA}$, that is $\frac{Hn_1}{4}$, or $\frac{x-5}{4}$, while the ordinate of $P_1 =$ that of $a_1 = 7 \sin \frac{x-5}{4}$; and similarly for any other point, P, on the curve.

Generally, then, to construct the curve

$$y = a \sin \frac{x-c}{b},$$

construct with any point C on the axis of x as centre a circle AB of radius b, and with the same centre a circle RS of radius a; from the origin O measure $OH = c$ in the positive direction if c is positive, and take HD equal to the half-circumference of the circle AB, proceed then as in the above numerical case.

If the curve had been given by $y = 7 \sin \dfrac{x+5}{4}$, the point H should have been taken 5 units to the left of the origin O, and the construction proceeded with as before.

The *amplitude* of the curve $y = a \sin \dfrac{x-c}{b}$ is the length of its greatest ordinate, viz., a; the *wave-length* is $2\pi b$, which is represented by HE in Fig. 25.

The term *phase* is also employed with regard to these curves It indicates the position of a point in the curve when the ordinates of the curve represent the displacements or velocities of a vibrating particle. Thus if from any point P_1 we draw a parallel to OX cutting the curve in P_1' and P_1'', although the ordinate of P_1' is equal to that of P_1 and of the same sign, the points P_1 and P_1' are not in the same phase, while P_1 and P_1'' are. The student will understand this better when he is employing the curve of sines as a graphic representation of a simple harmonic vibration. Our purpose here is sufficiently carried out by saying that two points on the curve are said to be in the same phase if their abscissæ x, x' differ by a whole wave-length, as do those of P_1 and P_1''.

We may call the circle RS the *amplitude circle*, and the circle AB the *wave-length circle*.

The curve $y = \cos x$ can, of course, be similarly constructed. It can be written $y = \sin (x - \tfrac{3}{2}\pi)$, and it can be drawn by taking in Fig. 25 the point H distant $\tfrac{3}{2}\pi$ from O in the positive direction, *i.e.*, at the foot of the ordinate of the point U in the figure, and proceeding as above.

Similarly the curve $y = 7 \cos \dfrac{x-5}{4}$ can be constructed by writing the equation in the form

$$y = 7 \sin \left(\frac{x-5}{4} - \tfrac{3}{2}\pi \right), \ i.e., \ y = 7 \sin \frac{x-5-6\pi}{4};$$

so that in Fig. 25 the point H is taken at a distance OH equal to $5 + 6\pi$, the rest being the same.

To superpose two curves of sines, *i e.*, to represent the curve

$$y = a \sin \frac{x-c}{b} + a' \sin \frac{x-c'}{b'},$$

we have merely to draw each curve exactly as above explained and for each abscissa add their ordinates algebraically.

As an example, we append the representation of the curve

$$y = 7 \sin \frac{x-5}{4} + 3 \sin \frac{x+4}{6}.$$

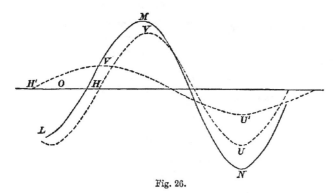

Fig. 26.

The origin of x is the point O; the dotted curve HVU is that whose amplitude and wave-length circles have radii 7 and 4; the dotted curve $H'V'U'$ is that whose circles have radii 3 and 6, and it starts at the point H' which is 4 units from O on the negative side.

The resultant curve LMN is not itself a curve of sines, a result due to the fact that the two curves from which it is deduced have not the same wave-length.

Superposition of curves of same wave-length. If we superpose the curves $y = a_1 \sin \frac{x-c_1}{b}$ and $y = a_2 \sin \frac{x-c_2}{b}$, in each of which the wave-length is $2\pi b$, we obtain a resultant curve of sines having this wave-length. For, put

$$y = a_1 \sin \frac{x-c_1}{b} + a_2 \sin \frac{x-c_2}{b}$$

$$= \left(a_1 \cos \frac{c_1}{b} + a_2 \cos \frac{c_2}{b}\right) \sin \frac{x}{b} - \left(a_1 \sin \frac{c_1}{b} + a_2 \sin \frac{c_2}{b}\right) \cos \frac{x}{b} \dots (1)$$

Now if we put

$$A \cos \frac{\gamma}{b} = a_1 \cos \frac{c_1}{b} + a_2 \cos \frac{c_2}{b}, \quad \dots\dots\dots\dots(2)$$

$$A \sin \frac{\gamma}{b} = a_1 \sin \frac{c_1}{b} + a_2 \sin \frac{c_2}{b}, \quad \dots\dots\dots\dots(3)$$

where A and γ are to be determined, (1) becomes

$$y = A \sin \frac{x - \gamma}{b}, \quad \dots \quad \dots\dots\dots(4)$$

which is a curve of sines of amplitude A and wave-length $2\pi b$.

A and γ are evidently given from (2) and (3) thus:

$$A = \sqrt{\left(\Sigma a \cos \frac{c}{b}\right)^2 + \left(\Sigma a \sin \frac{c}{b}\right)^2}, \quad \dots \quad \dots \dots(5)$$

$$\tan \frac{\gamma}{b} = \frac{\Sigma a \sin \frac{c}{b}}{\Sigma a \cos \frac{c}{b}}, \quad \dots\dots\dots\dots\dots\dots(6)$$

where Σ is used as a sign of summation.

Similarly if any number of curves of sines of the same wave-length are superposed so that

$$y = a_1 \sin \frac{x - c_1}{b} + a_2 \sin \frac{x - c_2}{b} + a_3 \sin \frac{x - c_3}{b} + \dots, \quad \dots(7)$$

we obtain a curve of sines

$$y = A \sin \frac{x - \gamma}{b}, \quad \dots\dots\dots\dots\dots(8)$$

where A, the resultant amplitude and γ the resultant phase-constant are given by (5) and (6).

It is obvious that in the equations

$$A \cos \frac{\gamma}{b} = a_1 \cos \frac{c_1}{b} + a_2 \cos \frac{c_2}{b} + a_3 \cos \frac{c_3}{b} + \dots, \quad \dots\dots(9)$$

$$A \sin \frac{\gamma}{b} = a_1 \sin \frac{c_1}{b} + a_2 \sin \frac{c_2}{b} + a_3 \sin \frac{c_3}{b} + \dots, \quad \dots(10)$$

we can regard the various amplitudes a_1, a_2, a_3, … as forces, or other vectors, drawn in directions making angles $\frac{c_1}{b}$, $\frac{c_2}{b}$, $\frac{c_3}{b}$, … with a fixed line, and then the resultant of these vectors is A, the resultant amplitude, while its direction determines $\frac{\gamma}{b}$.

Hence amplitudes and phases can be compounded, and also resolved, by any of the ordinary rules of vector composition and resolution—such as the parallelogram or the polygon of vectors.

To solve an equation of the form $a \sin \dfrac{x-c}{b} = f(x)$, *where* $f(x)$ *is a given function of* x.

Trace the curve $y = a \sin \dfrac{x-c}{b}$ and also the curve $y = f(x)$, and the required values of x are those belonging to their points of intersection.

EXAMPLES.

1. Find the values of x that satisfy the equation

$$7 \sin \frac{x-5}{4} = \frac{x}{2} - 1.$$

Here we draw the curve of sines HVU (Fig. 25) whose equation is $y = 7 \sin \dfrac{x-5}{4}$, and also the right line $y = \dfrac{x}{2} - 1$, and an inspection of the figure shows that they intersect in three points, whose abscissæ are roughly $-5\cdot5$, $6\cdot2$, and $13\cdot6$.

Now when we have an approximate value of x, Taylor's Theorem will give a more accurate one. Thus, to obtain a closer approximation than $13\cdot6$ to the last value of x, let $x = 13\cdot6 + \xi$ where ξ is a small quantity. Then

$$7 \sin \frac{13\cdot6 + \xi - 5}{4} = 5\cdot8 + \frac{\xi}{2}, \text{ or } 7 \sin \left(\frac{8\cdot6}{4} + \frac{\xi}{4} \right) = 5\cdot8 + \frac{\xi}{2}.$$

Expanding and retaining only the first power of ξ, we have

$$\xi \left(\frac{1}{2} - \frac{7}{4} \cos \frac{4\cdot3}{2} \right) = 7 \sin \frac{4\cdot3}{2} - 5\cdot8,$$

$$\therefore \xi = \cdot04,$$

and $x = 13\cdot64$ is the nearer value. Similarly the other two rough values can be corrected.

2. Solve the equation $3 \sin \dfrac{x+4}{6} = 4 + \frac{2}{3}x$.

The reading of the diagram gives $x = -9\cdot5$, about, a closer approximation being $x = -9\cdot6$.

3. Solve the equation $7 \sin \dfrac{x-5}{4} = x^2$.

There are no real solutions, because the parabola $y = x^2$ does not intersect $y = 7 \sin \dfrac{x-5}{4}$.

4. Solve the equation $7 \sin \dfrac{x-5}{4} + x^2 = 0$.

Result: $x = 2\cdot14$ and $x = -2\cdot58$ are the only solutions.

5. Find x from the equation $\alpha = x - e \sin x$, where α and e are given.

Construct the curves $y = \sin x$, $y = \dfrac{1}{e}(x - \alpha)$, the latter of which is a right line passing through a point (suppose N in Fig. 25) at a distance α from the origin and making the angle whose tangent is $\dfrac{1}{e}$ with the axis of x.

This is the solution of Kepler's problem: to find the position of a planet in its orbit at any assigned time. For a planet, however, e is so very small that the value of x would not differ visibly from α in the drawing. For a periodic comet the result would be different.

23. The Curve of Squares, $y = x^2$. In drawing curves it is sometimes desirable to adopt different scales in representing abscissæ and ordinates. In the case of the curve of squares, for example, if the same length represents a unit along the axis of x and along the axis of y, when $x = 3$, $y = 9$, and the ordinate may be inconveniently great; and the result is still worse if $x = 4, 5, \ldots$ To avoid this inconvenience, we represent a unit in the y direction by a very much smaller length than that which represents a unit in the x direction. Thus if in Fig. 27 we take one side of a small square to represent a unit of y and five sides to represent a unit of x, we are enabled to represent a considerable portion of the curve, AOB, which, of course, is a parabola.

Having drawn this curve of squares, we can now draw very rapidly, on the same or any other scale, the curve whose ordinates are the squares of the ordinates of any assigned curve, these ordinates being all measured from the same line Ox.

Thus, let it be required to draw the squares of the ordinates of the circle $SPQR$: take any ordinate NP; if NP contains n of the

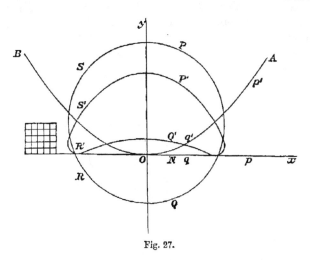

Fig. 27.

y units, to get NP^2 we must measure on Ox a length containing n of the x units—that is, we must take a length OZ (not shown in the figure) along Ox equal to five times the length NP, since each x unit has been taken to contain five of the y units; then at the point Z erect an ordinate to the parabola BOA, and this ordinate is the square of NP. But it is not necessary to measure the length OZ; we can take one-fifth of it, or any other fraction; we may simply take $Op = NP$, and the ordinate pp' of the parabola corresponding to the point p is $\frac{1}{25}$ of the ordinate of the point Z, since $Op = \frac{1}{5}OZ$, that is the square of NP is 25 times pp'. Measure $NP' = pp'$, and do this for all points, $P, Q, R, S, \ldots$ on the circle, and we obtain a curve, $P'Q'R'S', \ldots$ *whose ordinates are $\frac{1}{25}$ of the squares of the ordinates of the circle.*

We might have measured $Op = 2NP$, and then the ordinate pp' would be $\frac{4}{25}$ of NP^2, and so on. Generally, if the x unit is m times the y unit, and we take $Op = n \cdot NP$, the ordinates of the curve $P'Q'R'S', \ldots$ will be $\dfrac{n^2}{m^2}$ times the squares of the ordinates of $PQRS$.

24. The Curve of Cubes, $y = x^3$. If, in the same way, taking five of the small divisions to represent a unit along Ox, and one division a unit along Oy, we construct the cubes of the values of x, we obtain the curve of cubes, Fig. 28. Any right line drawn in the plane of this curve must meet it in *one* real point at least, and may meet it in three, of which two may be coincident.

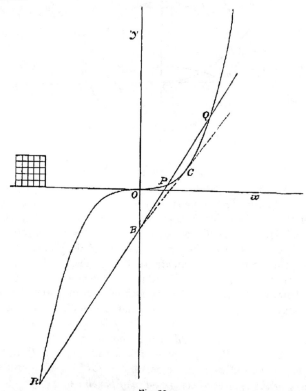

Fig. 28.

To solve the cubic $ax^3 + bx^2 + cx + d = 0$. Remove the second term by the well-known method, and let the equation then be

$$x^3 + qx + r = 0.$$

To solve this, construct the curves

$$y = x^3, \dots\dots\dots\dots\dots\dots\dots\dots\dots(1)$$
$$y = -qx - r. \dots\dots\dots\dots\dots\dots(2)$$

The second is a right line making intercepts $-\dfrac{r}{q}$ and $-r$ on the axes of x and $y.$ '

Suppose r to be positive; then if $OB = r$ in Fig. 28, the line (2) is some line passing through B. Now if this line cuts Ox at the negative side, it cannot meet the curve (1) in more than one real point. Hence if the three roots are real, the intercept $-\dfrac{r}{q}$ must be positive, *i.e.*, q must be negative.

If r is negative, the point B is above 0, and for real intersections of the line (2) with the cube curve, the intercept $-\dfrac{r}{q}$ must be negative, *i.e.*, q must be negative—as before. For the existence of *three* real roots, therefore, q must be negative.

To find more definitely the condition for three real roots, let BC be the tangent from B to the curve; then any line through B cutting the curve in three real points must lie to the left of BC. The equation of the tangent at C is $y - y' = 3x'^2 (x - x')$, where x', y' are the co-ordinates of C. Since this tangent passes through B, put $y = -r$, $x = 0$; then $-r - y' = -3x'^3$, $\therefore y' = \dfrac{r}{2}$ and $x' = \left(\dfrac{r}{2}\right)^{\frac{1}{3}}$. Now the tangent of the angle which BC makes with Ox is $3x'^2$, *i.e.*, $3\left(\dfrac{r^2}{4}\right)^{\frac{1}{3}}$; and the tangent of the angle which the line $y = -qx - r$ makes with Ox is $-q$.

Hence for real intersections

$$-q > 3\left(\frac{r^2}{4}\right)^{\frac{1}{3}},$$

or $\qquad\qquad \dfrac{r^2}{4} + \dfrac{q^3}{27}$ is negative,

which is the well-known condition deduced in the theory of equations. Similarly, if r is negative, the line BPQ meets the curve in three real points, and if the line coincides with BC, two roots are equal, each equal to the x of C. The condition for equal roots is $\dfrac{r^2}{4} + \dfrac{q^3}{27} = 0.$

From the figure we have deduced the fact that, for the existence of three real roots, q must be negative; but this is at once seen by algebra. For if α, β, γ are the roots of a cubic,

$$x^3 + px^2 + qx + r = 0,$$

we have $\alpha + \beta + \gamma = -p$, and $\alpha\beta + \beta\gamma + \gamma\alpha = q$,

$$\therefore \ \alpha^2 + \beta^2 + \gamma^2 = p^2 - 2q.$$

Now if $\alpha + \beta + \gamma = 0$, we have

$$q = -\tfrac{1}{2}(\alpha^2 + \beta^2 + \gamma^2),$$

and if α, β, γ are any real quantities, the right-hand side must be negative, therefore q is $-$.

To solve the biquadratic, $ax^4 + bx^3 + cx^2 + dx + e = 0$. Remove the second term, and let the equation become $x^4 + qx^2 + rx + s = 0$. This can be written $\left(x^2 + \dfrac{q}{2}\right)^2 + rx + s - \dfrac{q^2}{4} = 0$. Now construct the curves

$$y = \left(x^2 + \frac{q}{2}\right)^2, \quad \dots\dots\dots\dots\dots\dots\dots(3)$$

$$y = -rx - s + \frac{q^2}{4}. \quad \dots\dots\dots\dots\dots\dots(4)$$

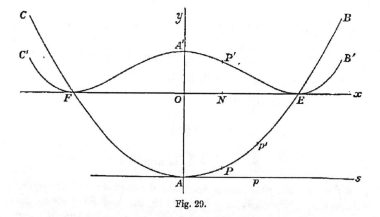

Fig. 29.

The curve (3) is obtained by constructing the parabola $y = x^2$, increasing each of its ordinates by $\tfrac{1}{2}q$, and from the parabola thus obtained deducing the curve whose ordinates are the squares of the ordinates of the new parabola. The parabola $y = x^2$ touches Ox at O, and the quantity $\frac{1}{2}q$ may be positive or negative. If q is positive, the curve $y = x^2 + \frac{1}{2}q$ is simply the parabola $y = x^2$ moved upwards by a motion of translation $\frac{1}{2}q$ perpendicular to Ox. If q is negative, the parabola $y = x^2 + \frac{1}{2}q$ is the parabola $y = x^2$ moved downwards from Ox through a distance numerically equal to $\frac{1}{2}q$. This is the supposition shown in the figure, in which OA is $\frac{1}{2}q$, and the displaced parabola is BAC. The curve (3) whose ordinates are the squares of those of BAC—the ordinates being, of course, measured from Ox—is $B'A'C'$, described exactly as in Art. 23; that is to say, let NP be any ordinate of BAC; measure $Ap = NP$, and let pp' be the ordinate of BAC measured from As; then erect the ordinate NP' equal to pp', and we have a point on the required curve (3).

The points in which this curve is cut by the right line (4) give the solutions of the equation

$$x^4 + qx^2 + rx + s = 0,$$

and we see that the whole four may be real.

But if q is positive, the parabola BAC lies above Ox, and the shape of the curve (3) is quite altered. This curve has no undulatory portion like $FA'E$; it is more or less parabolic in form, and no right line can meet it in four real points.

As before, the fact that q must be negative when there are four real roots is evident algebraically. For an equation of any degree, $x^n + p_1 x^{n-1} + p_2 x^{n-2} + \ldots = 0$, the sum of the squares of the roots is $p_1^2 - 2p_2$, so that the sum of the squares of the roots of $x^n + qx^{n-2} + \ldots = 0$ is $-2q$; and therefore q must be negative if all the roots are real.

Professor Loney solves the biquadratic in the following way. Let the equation be $x^4 + 4a_1 x^3 + 6a_2 x^2 + 4a_3 x + a_4 = 0$. Construct the parabola $y = x^2 + 2ax + \lambda$, and the circle $x^2 + y^2 + 2px = r$. Eliminating y from these curves, we obtain the given biquadratic, provided that

$$\lambda = 3a_2 - 2a_1^2 - \tfrac{1}{2}; \quad p = 2a_3 - 3a_1 a_2 - 2a_1^3 - \tfrac{1}{2}a_1;$$
$$r = (3a_2 - 2a_1^2 - \tfrac{1}{2})^2 - a_4;$$

so that the roots are given by the intersections of the parabola and the circle.

If we begin by depriving the biquadratic of its second term, the result is presented in a simple form. Thus, if the biquadratic is $x^4 + qx^2 + rx + s = 0$, the parabola and circle are

$$y - \tfrac{1}{2}(1-q) = x^2 \,; \quad \left(x + \frac{r}{2}\right)^2 + y^2 = \tfrac{1}{4}\left[(1-q)^2 + r^2 - 4s\right].$$

Both of these curves are easily constructed; for, as in the other solution, the parabola is simply the curve of squares moved parallel to the axis of y through a distance $\tfrac{1}{2}(1-q)$.

EXAMPLES.

1. Solve the equation $x^4 - 4x^3 - 31x^2 + 94x + 120 = 0$.

Removing the second term, the equation becomes

$$x^4 - 37x^2 + 24x + 180 = 0.$$

Writing this in the form $(x^2 - \tfrac{37}{2})^2 + 24x - \tfrac{849}{4} = 0$, construct the curve $y = (x^2 - \tfrac{37}{2})^2$, from the parabola CAB (Fig. 29), placing the origin O at a distance $\tfrac{37}{2}$ units of y above A. Derive the curve $FA'E$ by measuring $Ap = NP$, and $NP' = pp'$, so that the ordinates of $FA'E$ are $\tfrac{1}{25}$ of the numerical values of $(x^2 - \tfrac{37}{2})^2$. We must, of course, similarly diminish the ordinates of the right line $y = -24x + \tfrac{849}{4}$; that is, we are to construct the line $y = \tfrac{1}{25}(-24x + \tfrac{849}{4})$. This line makes intercepts 6·49 of the y units on Oy and 6·76 of the x units along Ox. Drawing the line, we see that it cuts the curve $FA'E$ in points whose abscissæ are 5, 3, -2, and -6; so that the roots of the given equation are 6, 4, -1, -5.

Mr Loney's parabola and circle are

$$y - 19 = x^2, \text{ and } (x + 12)^2 + y^2 = 325.$$

2. Find the real roots of $x^4 - 2x^3 - 5x^2 - 6x - 24 = 0$.

They are 4 and -2.

3. Find the real roots of the equation

$$x^4 + 20x^2 + 35x - 75 = 0.$$

From the figure we read, as nearly as possible, $x = 1·2$ and $x = -2·5$, from which more correct values are obtained by Taylor's theorem.

4. Show by graphic construction that the equation

$$x^4 - hx^3 + 1 = 0$$

has, for all values of h, at least two imaginary roots, and find the smallest value of h for which it has two real roots.

The smallest value of h is $\frac{4}{9} \cdot \sqrt[4]{3}$.

25. The Logarithmic Curve and the Catenary. Taking two rectangular axes, Ox, Oy (Fig. 30), construct the curve whose equation is

$$y = e^x. \quad \text{..............................(1)}$$

This is called the logarithmic curve. The curve, $BQAD$, cuts Oy at the point A such that $OA = 1$; and the curve approaches the line Ox asymptotically. It has been plotted from Dale's *Mathematical Tables*, p. 64.

We may take the equation in its general and homogeneous form,

$$y = be^{\frac{x}{a}}, \quad \text{..............................(2)}$$

where a and b are any two constant lengths, and the nature of the curve will be the same. In the figure the unit length along Oy has been taken the same as that along Ox. These might have been made different; thus we might have taken a side of a large

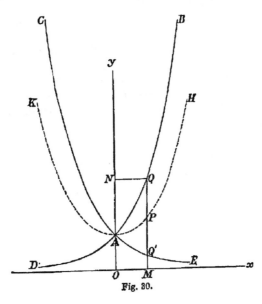

Fig. 30.

square (Fig. 28) as a unit of x and a side of one of the smallest squares as a unit of y; and the effect would be to draw the curve BQA much farther away to the right. The curve CAE is the curve BAD rotated through two right angles about Oy.

If N is the foot of the perpendicular from a point Q, of the curve on Oy, we have $NQ = \log ON$, i.e., the ordinates measured perpendicularly to Oy are the logarithms of the corresponding values of y.

The curve whose equation is

$$y = \tfrac{1}{2}(e^x + e^{-x}) \ldots \ldots \ldots \ldots \ldots \ldots \ldots (3)$$

is a Catenary; and this curve is obviously obtained by drawing ordinates, $QQ'M, \ldots$ cutting BAD and CAE in Q and $Q', \ldots$, and taking $MP = \tfrac{1}{2}(MQ + MQ')$, i.e., P is the middle point of QQ'. The Catenary thus derived is $HPAK$, its parameter is 1, and its directrix is Ox, OA being equal to 1. If the curve BAD had been drawn so that the unit of $y = \dfrac{1}{n}$ of the unit of x, is a Catenary obtained by this process? No: we obtain thus a curve BAD whose ordinate is in reality only $\dfrac{1}{n}e^x$, and the derived curve, HPA, has for equation $y = \dfrac{1}{2n}(e^x + e^{-x})$, which is not a Catenary.

From any one given Catenary all Catenaries can be constructed, since all Catenaries are similar curves. For, let c be any constant length; then the general form of the equation of the Catenary is

$$y = \frac{c}{2}\left(e^{\frac{x}{c}} + e^{-\frac{x}{c}}\right), \ldots \ldots \ldots \ldots \ldots \ldots (4)$$

c being the *parameter* of the curve. Let this curve be mAn in Fig. 31, $O'A$ being c, and $O'd$ the directrix, from which y in (4) is measured.

Let it be required to construct the Catenary whose parameter is b, and let $OA = b$. This second Catenary has for its equation, referred to OD as axis of x,

$$Y = \frac{b}{2}\left(e^{\frac{X}{b}} + e^{-\frac{X}{b}}\right), \ldots \ldots \ldots \ldots \ldots \ldots (5)$$

which can be written in the form

$$\frac{c}{b} Y = \frac{c}{2} \left(e^{\frac{c}{b}\frac{x}{c}} + e^{-\frac{c}{b}\frac{x}{c}} \right). \quad \dots \dots \dots \dots (6)$$

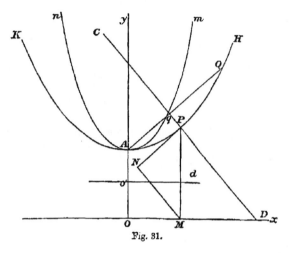

Fig. 31.

Now this is the same as (4) if

$$\frac{Y}{b} = \frac{y}{c} \quad \text{and} \quad \frac{X}{b} = \frac{x}{c}. \quad \dots \dots \dots \dots (7)$$

Let q be the point (x, y) on the first Catenary, and Q the point (X, Y) on the second. Then (7) assert that OQ is parallel to $O'q$, and that

$$\frac{OQ}{O'q} = \frac{b}{c} = \frac{OA}{O'A}, \quad \dots \dots \dots \dots (8)$$

that is AqQ is one right line, and

$$AQ = \frac{b}{c} \cdot Aq, \quad \dots \dots \dots \dots (9)$$

so that the new Catenary is obtained simply by increasing the radii vectores $Aq, \dots$ of the first in the ratio $b:c$.

Thus from the Catenary (3) whose parameter is 1 can be deduced all others.

The right-hand side of (3) is the hyperbolic cosine of x,

denoted by cosh x—or, better, ch x*; so that the curve (3) may be written

$$y = \text{ch } x. \quad \dots\dots\dots\dots\dots\dots\dots(10)$$

The Catenary is the curve formed by a uniform flexible chain when its ends are fixed and the chain hangs freely under the action of gravity. No *string* will form a Catenary, because a string is a comparatively rigid body: a chain of small uniform links is the realization of the curve.

The curve $y = \text{ch } x$ may be taken as represented by mAn, the length AO' being a unit both for x and for y.

The curve $y = \frac{1}{2}(e^x - e^{-x})$ is obtained by erecting at each point M on Ox an ordinate equal to $\frac{1}{2}Q'Q$ in Fig 30. The expression $\frac{1}{2}(e^x - e^{-x})$ is called the *hyperbolic sine* of x, and is denoted by sh x. Fig. 32 thus obtained, or plotted from Dale's *Mathematical Tables*, represents the curve $y = \text{sh } x$.

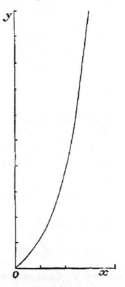

Fig. 32.

* Some of the hyperbolic functions, such as sinh, tanh, sech, &c., have unpronounceable names; hence they are better denoted by sh, th, sch. When they have to be spoken of, they might with advantage be called

hysin, hytan, hysec, &c.,

which are sufficiently simple and euphonious.

Only the positive half of the curve is here represented : there is an exactly similar portion of the curve at the negative sides of Ox and Oy, since $\operatorname{sh}(-x) = -\operatorname{sh} x$.

Prominent properties of the Catenary. The following properties of the Catenary should be known, although they are not all very directly concerned with the present subject.

1. Given any two fixed points, H, K, if a curve of *given length* connects them, the centre of gravity of this curve (considered as a thin uniform chain) will be farthest from the line HK when the curve is part of a Catenary.

Hence of all curves of the same length generating surfaces of revolution by revolving round the line HK, the Catenary is the curve which generates the surface of greatest area. (See Theorems of Pappus in treatises on Statics, Calculus, &c.)

2. If the tangent PN is drawn at any point P of the Catenary, and a perpendicular, MN, is let fall on it from the foot, M, of the ordinate (measured from the directrix), the length MN is constant and equal to OA, or c, the parameter of the Catenary. Also the length, s, of the arc AP of the curve is equal to PN, so that if $y = PM$, we have

$$y^2 = s^2 + c^2 \quad \dots\dots\dots\dots\dots\dots\dots(11)$$

for all points on the curve. The value of s in terms of x is obtained therefore by changing the sign of $e^{-\frac{x}{c}}$ in (4), and we have

$$s = c \operatorname{sh} \frac{x}{c}, \quad \dots\dots\dots\dots\dots\dots(12)$$

where $\operatorname{sh} \dfrac{x}{c}$ means $\frac{1}{2}\left(e^{\frac{x}{c}} - e^{-\frac{x}{c}}\right)$, the hyperbolic sine of $\dfrac{x}{c}$.

In the triangle MPN, we have then

$$PM = c \operatorname{ch} \frac{x}{c}; \quad PN = c \operatorname{sh} \frac{x}{c}; \quad MN = c. \quad \dots\dots\dots(13)$$

The facts that the arc $AP = PN$ and that $MN = OA$ are a very useful help to the student in drawing a freehand figure of the Catenary. Of course he will be careful to observe that the tangent can never become parallel to the line Oy, since if θ is the angle which the tangent makes with Ox

$$\tan \theta = \frac{s}{c}, \quad \dots\dots\dots\dots\dots\dots(14)$$

which shows that θ can never reach a right angle until $s = \infty$.

The radius of curvature PC at each point P is equal to the length PD of the normal intercepted by the directrix, the centre of curvature, C, and the foot, D, of the normal being on opposite sides of the tangent at P.

4. The Catenary is in shape very like the Parabola, and was supposed to be one by Galileo. If we consider points in the neighbourhood of the vertex for which x is less than c, and expand the exponentials in (4), we have

$$y = c \left\{ 1 + \frac{x^2}{2c^2} + \frac{x^4}{24c^4} + \cdots \right\},$$

in which, of course, y is measured from Ox. If y is measured from the tangent at A, we shall have

$$y = \frac{x^2}{2c}, \text{ or } x^2 = 2cy, \quad \ldots\ldots\ldots\ldots(15)$$

if we neglect $\left(\frac{x}{c}\right)^4$; which shows the closeness of the figure to that of the parabola. In Telegraphy the wire stretching from post to post is always taken as forming a parabola, and justly so because it is a Catenary in which the parameter c is enormously large compared with the semi-span, which is the largest value of x involved; for example if the span is 150 feet and the central sag is 1 foot, the parameter c is more than half a mile.

5 The length of the arc PQ connecting any two points on the curve may be expressed in terms of the *horizontal* and *vertical* distances between P and Q. Let the co-ordinates of Q be (x', y'), and let those of P be (x, y); then, Q and P being at the same side of Oy, the horizontal distance between them is $x' - x$, and the vertical distance $y' - y$. Denote these distances by h and k, respectively, and let $l =$ the length of the arc PQ; then the student may prove the following equation:

$$c \left(e^{\frac{h}{2c}} - e^{-\frac{h}{2c}} \right) = \sqrt{l^2 - k^2}. \quad \ldots\ldots\ldots\ldots(16)$$

If Q and P are at opposite sides of Oy, h in this equation will be the arithmetical *sum* of their distances from Oy.

6. If a uniform chain hangs over two smooth supports, H, K, fixed in a horizontal line, the ends of the chain being free, these

ends must both lie on the directrix, Ox, of the Catenary, and if $2l$ is the whole length of this chain, we have

$$l = ce^{\frac{a}{c}}, \dots\dots\dots\dots\dots\dots \text{(17)}$$

where the span, HK, is $2a$. This follows at once by adding the s and the y of the point H. Whether the two smooth fixed supports are in the same horizontal line or not, the ends of the freely hanging parts must both lie on the directrix.

7. If a uniform chain hangs freely under the action of gravity, and y is the ordinate of any point measured from the directrix of the Catenary, the tension at that point is equal to the weight of a length y of the chain; so that if w is the weight per unit length of the chain, this tension is $w.y$.

This is true no matter how the chain is suspended. Its ends may be fixed at any two points which are not in the same horizontal line, or it may hang with free extremities by passing over two smooth pegs fixed occupying any positions.

CATENARY EXAMPLES.

1. Calculate the Catenary formed by a uniform chain 30 feet long having a horizontal span of 20 feet.

If HK is the span (Fig. 31), and the curve is HAK, we have

$$\text{arc } AH = 15 = c \text{ sh } \frac{10}{c},$$

where c is the required parameter of the Catenary.

To solve this, let $\frac{10}{c} = x$; then the equation becomes $\frac{3}{2}x = \text{sh } x$.

Hence we construct the curves

$$y = \tfrac{3}{2}x \text{ and } y = \text{sh } x.$$

The first is a right line, and the second the curve in Fig. 32. Drawing the right line, we see that it cuts the curve near the point for which $x = 1.6$. To obtain a closer approximation, let $x = 1.6 + \zeta$; then we have, neglecting powers of ζ beyond the first,

$$\tfrac{3}{2}(1.6 + \zeta) = \text{sh } (1.6 + \zeta) = \text{sh } (1.6) + \zeta \text{ ch } (1.6).$$

From Dale's Tables we have

$$\text{sh } (1.6) = 2.37557 ; \quad \text{ch } (1.6) = 2.57746 ;$$

hence $\qquad\qquad\qquad \zeta = 0.23,$

$$\therefore \quad x = 1.623, \quad \therefore \quad c = 6.16.$$

If y is the ordinate of H, $y = \sqrt{15^2 + (6\cdot16)^2} = 16\cdot22$, nearly; and the depth of the curve, *i.e.*, the depth of the vertex below HK is $y - c$, or $10\cdot06$ feet.

2. If the length of the Catenary is $2l$ and the span $2a$, calculate the curve.

Here we have $l = c \operatorname{sh} \dfrac{a}{c}$. Let $\dfrac{a}{c} = x$, and we have to find x from the equation $\dfrac{l}{a} x = \operatorname{sh} x$. We have therefore the curves

$$y = \frac{l}{a} x ; \quad y = \operatorname{sh} x.$$

It is obvious that unless $\dfrac{l}{a}$ is considerably greater than unity we shall get no very clear value of x from Fig. 32, because the tangent at O to the hyperbolic sine curve makes an angle of 45° with Ox. In cases in which l is very little greater than a—as, for example, telegraph lines—c is very large, and it is better to expand the exponentials in the equation $l = \dfrac{c}{2} \left(e^{\frac{a}{c}} - e^{-\frac{a}{c}} \right)$. If we do this, we have

$$l = a + \tfrac{1}{6} \frac{a^3}{c^2} + \tfrac{1}{120} \frac{a^5}{c^4} + \cdots .$$

Let $\dfrac{a}{c}$ be denoted by x, and this becomes, if we neglect powers beyond the fifth,

$$x^4 + 20x^2 - 120 \left(\frac{l}{a} - 1 \right) = 0,$$

which gives
$$x^2 = \sqrt{120 \frac{l}{a} - 20} - 10.$$

3. A uniform wire 102 feet long has its ends fixed at two points, H, K, in a horizontal line 100 feet apart; find the Catenary, and the sag in the middle.

Here the graphic construction does not help. The parameter c is $158\cdot51$ feet, and the central sag (depth of vertex below HK) is 8 feet—a result which may strike the student as incredible. Let him, however, consider that the second side of a right-angled triangle whose hypotenuse is 51 and one side 50 is $\sqrt{101}$ feet; and obviously the central sag of the wire in this question must be only a little less than this.

4. Solve the equation $4x = e^x$.

Construct the curves $y = 4x$ and $y = e^x$. The latter is the curve BQA, Fig. 30; and the right line intersects it in points for which x seems to be ·36 and 2·1.

Taking the former, let $x = 36 + \zeta$; then, taking the value of e^x from Dale's Tables, p. 64,

$$1\cdot44 + 4\zeta = 1\cdot4333\,(1 + \zeta),$$

$$\therefore \quad \zeta = -\cdot0026, \quad \therefore \quad x = \cdot357.$$

In the same way, taking the second value, we get $\zeta = -\cdot056$, $\therefore x = 2\cdot044$.

This is the expression of the following problem: a uniform chain 24 inches long hangs with free extremities over two smooth supports, H, K, Fig. 31, whose distance apart is 6 inches; find the figures of equilibrium. In equation (17), p. 47, put $l = 12$, $a = 3$, and we have $12 = ce^{\frac{3}{c}}$. Let $\frac{3}{c} = x$, and we get $4x = e^x$. There are, therefore, two values of c and therefore two Catenaries, whose parameters are about 8·4 and 1·46 inches: a deep Catenary and a shallow one.

5. Solve the equation $\dfrac{l}{a}\,x = e^x$, where l and a are given.

Construct the curves $y = \dfrac{l}{a}x$, $y = e^x$. Then it is obvious from Fig. 30 that there are two points of intersection or none according as the right line lies above or below the tangent drawn from O to the curve AQB. To find this tangent, let it touch AQB at the point (x', y'); then the equation of the tangent is

$$y - y' = e^{x'}\,(x - x'),$$

and since this tangent passes through O, we have $y' = e^{x'} . x'$, $\therefore x' = 1$ and $y' = e$. Hence if $OM = 1$, OP is the tangent from O, and this tangent makes with Ox an angle whose tangent is e, so that the line $y = \dfrac{l}{a}x$ will cut the curve if $\dfrac{l}{a} > e$.

This is the expression of the following problem: a uniform chain of total length $2l$ hangs, with free extremities, over two smooth supports in a horizontal line at a distance $2a$ apart; find the figure of equilibrium.

M. D.   4

We see that there are either *two* figures or none according as the whole length of the chain is greater or less than about $2\frac{3}{4}$ times the span (accurately $2\cdot71828\ldots$ times the span).

6. A uniform chain of length 50 feet is to have its extremities fixed at two points in the same horizontal line; find their distance apart so that the tension at each support shall be three times the tension at the lowest point.

Let y and c be the ordinates of the highest and lowest point, measured from the directrix; then $y = 3c$. Also $y^2 = 25^2 + c^2$,

$\therefore\ c = \dfrac{25}{2\sqrt{2}}$, and if $2a$ is the span, we can now find a from either of the equations

$$y = c\,\mathrm{ch}\left(\frac{a}{c}\right),\ \ \text{or}\ \ s = l = c\,\mathrm{sh}\left(\frac{a}{c}\right),$$

or more simply by adding l and y; for $l + y = ce^{\frac{a}{c}}$.

Hence $\qquad\qquad e^{\frac{a}{c}} = 3 + 2\sqrt{2}.$

Taking the logarithm of each side,

$$\cdot4343 \times \frac{a}{c} = \log 5\cdot8284 = \cdot7655,$$

$$\therefore\quad a = 15\cdot58,\ \ \therefore\ \ \text{span} = 31\cdot16\ \text{feet}.$$

7. For the same length of chain find the span when each terminal tension is 5 times the tension at the lowest point.

Span $= 16\cdot21$.

8. It is required to describe a Catenary whose length is 65 feet through two points, Q, P, Fig. 31, whose horizontal and vertical distances apart are 20 and 56 feet, respectively.

In equation (16), p. 46 we have $h = 20$, $l = 65$, $k = 56$, therefore we have to find c from the equation

$$c\left(e^{\frac{10}{c}} - e^{-\frac{10}{c}}\right) = 33.$$

Put $\dfrac{10}{c} = x$, and this becomes

$$\mathrm{sh}\,(x) = \tfrac{33}{20}x. \quad\ldots\ldots\ldots\ldots\ldots\ldots\ldots(a)$$

Construct the curves $y = \mathrm{sh}\,(x)$, $y = \tfrac{33}{20}x$, Fig. 32. The right line meets the curve in a point for which $x = 1\cdot8$, about. Let $x = 1\cdot8 + \zeta$; then (a) gives

$$\mathrm{sh}\,(1\cdot8) + \zeta\,\mathrm{ch}\,(1\cdot8) = \tfrac{33}{20}(1\cdot8 + \zeta),$$

and from Dale's Tables we get $\zeta = \dfrac{\cdot 02783}{1\cdot 45747} = \cdot 019$; hence $c = 5\cdot 5$, nearly, which determines the Catenary. Thus, to find the position of the lowest point, A, let $y =$ height of P above directrix, $s =$ arc AP; then we have

$$(y + 56)^2 = (s + 65)^2 + (5\cdot 5)^2,$$
$$y^2 = s^2 + (5\cdot 5)^2,$$
$$\therefore\ 112y - 130s = 33^2,$$

and we obtain $s = -2\cdot 99$, which shows that the lowest point of the Catenary is in the part between Q and P. Also $y = 6\cdot 26$, which is the depth of the directrix below P.

The problem, therefore, to find the Catenary of given length which passes through two points which are not in the same horizontal line leads to exactly the same equation as if the points were in a horizontal line—viz., an equation of the form

$$\mathrm{sh}\,(x) = nx,$$

where n is given.

DIPOLAR CO-ORDINATES.

Angles.

26. **Dipolar Angles.** If A and B are two fixed points, the position of a point P is sometimes determined by the angles

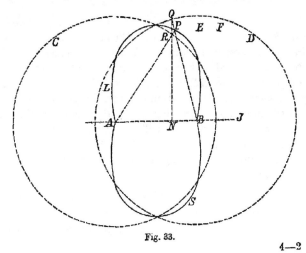

Fig. 33.

4—2

PAB and PBA. These angles θ, ϕ, constitute what are called dipolar co-ordinates. The distances PA and PB may also be used as co-ordinates of P.

27. The Magnetic Curve. Given the base and the sum of the cosines of the base angles of a triangle, the locus of the vertex is a curve called the *Magnetic Curve*. This curve can be constructed in the following manner.

Let k be the given sum of cosines, so that if P is any position of the vertex, and the angles PAB and PBA are θ and ϕ, respectively, we have

$$\cos \theta + \cos \phi = k. \quad \dots\dots\dots\dots\dots\dots(1)$$

About A as centre describe a circle, C, of radius $\dfrac{AB}{k}$, and about B describe a circle, D, of equal radius. Draw any perpendicular, QRN, to AB meeting the circles R and Q; draw AR and BQ intersecting in P. Then this point is a point on the required locus; for,

$$\cos PAB = \frac{AN}{AR}, \text{ and } \cos PBA = \frac{BN}{BQ}, \therefore \cos PAB + \cos PBA = \frac{AB}{AR},$$

since $AR = BQ$; and since $AR = \dfrac{AB}{k}$, we have

$$\cos PAB + \cos PBA = k,$$

so that the angles PAB and PBA, and all angles similarly determined, satisfy (1). The points P which are thus determined by drawing all perpendiculars to AB trace out the curve $PBSAL$, which is symmetrical with respect to AB and also with respect to the perpendicular to AB at its middle point. It is called the magnetic curve, because if A and B are the poles of a magnet, and small iron filings are shaken on the plane of the paper, a small straight filing at P will set itself along the tangent to this curve at P, so that we can see strings of filings setting themselves tangentially along a series of curves obtained by varying k in (1).

Given the base and the difference of the cosines of the base angles of a triangle, construct the locus of the vertex.

This is done by a slight modification of the previous construction.

Measure any length BN from B towards A, and an equal length BN' from B in the opposite direction; let the ordinate

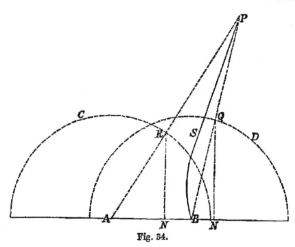

Fig. 34.

at N meet the circle C described round A as centre with radius $\dfrac{AB}{k}$ in R, and let the ordinate at N' meet the circle D, of same radius with B as centre, in Q; then AR and BQ meet in a point P which satisfies the equation

$$\cos \theta - \cos \phi = k. \quad\quad\quad\quad\quad\quad\quad (2)$$

For,

$$\cos \theta = \frac{AN}{AR}, \; \cos \phi = -\frac{BN'}{BQ}; \; \therefore \cos \theta - \cos \phi = \frac{AN + BN'}{AR} = k,$$

by construction.

The curve thus traced out in this way is PSB. At the point B the value of θ is 0, and ϕ is the angle which the tangent at B makes with AB, viz., $\cos^{-1}(1-k)$. Portions of the locus below AB are easily drawn by taking the intersections of the ordinates with the lower parts of the circles. (The value of k for which the figure is drawn is $\frac{1}{4}$.)

Another method of constructing this curve consists in deriving it from the magnetic curve thus: take any point, P, on the magnetic curve, Fig. 33; from P let fall a perpendicular, PE, on the line BE which is drawn at B at right angles to AB;

produce PE to F so that $PE = FE$; then the line BF intersects AP in a point P' on the curve (2), because the angle

$$FBA = \pi - PBA,$$

and therefore $P'AB$ and $P'BA$ are values of θ and ϕ satisfying (2). We can also use the magnetic curve as representing (2) if the external angle PBJ is taken as ϕ.

Given the base, AB, of a triangle and $m \cos \theta \pm n \cos \phi = k$, where m, n, k are positive constants; construct the locus of the vertex.

First let

$$m \cos \theta + n \cos \phi = k. \quad \dots\dots\dots\dots\dots\dots(3)$$

With A as centre (Fig. 33) and radius $\dfrac{m}{k} AB$ describe a circle C; with B as centre and radius $\dfrac{n}{k} AB$ describe a circle D; draw any ordinate QRN meeting C and D in R and Q respectively; then the intersection, P, of AR and BQ is a point on the required locus.

For,

$$\cos \theta = \frac{AN}{AR} = \frac{k}{m} \cdot \frac{AN}{AB}; \quad \cos \phi = \frac{BN}{BQ} = \frac{k}{n} \cdot \frac{BN}{AB};$$

$$\therefore \; m \cos \theta + n \cos \phi = \frac{AN + BN}{AB} \cdot k = k,$$

whatever be the position of N.

The curve is a generalization of the magnetic curve—a kind of deformed magnetic curve.

Secondly, let

$$m \cos \theta - n \cos \phi = k. \quad \dots\dots\dots\dots\dots\dots(4)$$

In Fig. 34 describe about A and B circles, C, D, of radii $\dfrac{m}{k} AB$ and $\dfrac{n}{k} AB$, just as above; take two points N, N' equidistant from B on opposite sides; at these points draw ordinates meeting the circles C and D in R and Q; then the lines AR and BQ intersect in a point on the locus. The proof is obvious.

Also the curve (4) can be deduced from the curve (3) by the method already explained for the case in which m and n are unity; we can, in fact, regard the internal angle PAB and the external angle PBJ as θ and ϕ in (4).

The shapes of these curves vary very much with the values of m, n, k. Thus (3) will have branches extending to infinity if ϕ can be equal to $\pi - \theta$, which it can be if k is numerically $< m - n$.

To represent as dipolar angles all values of θ and ϕ satisfying the equation

$$m \sin \theta + n \sin \phi = k. \quad \dots\dots\dots\dots\dots(5)$$

Of course all values of θ and ϕ satisfying this equation are already represented by the construction of (3) above. For if in Fig. 33 the curve $PBSAL$ represents by all such angles as PAB and PBA the values of θ and ϕ satisfying (3), it is evident that the angles which PA and PB make with any perpendicular to AB are angles satisfying (5).

If we wish to represent θ and ϕ as angles at A and B made with AB by lines PA and PB, we can adopt the following construction.

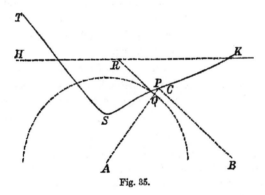

Fig. 35.

Take any two points, A, B; draw a line HK parallel to AB at any distance, h, from it; about A as centre describe a circle of radius $\frac{m}{k}h$; take a pair of dividers opened to a distance $\frac{n}{k}h$ between the points; take any point, Q, on the circle, and with the dividers inflect the length QR equal to $\frac{n}{k}h$, thus determining a point R on HK; through B draw a parallel, BP, to QR; then AQ meets BP in a point P on the required locus of P.

For, if y is the ordinate of Q measured from AB,

$$\sin QAB = \frac{y}{AQ} = \frac{k}{m} \cdot \frac{y}{h}; \quad \text{and} \quad \sin QRK = \frac{h-y}{QR} = \frac{k}{n} \cdot \frac{h-y}{h}.$$

This angle QRK is equal to PBA. Hence if $\theta = PAB$ and $\phi = PBA$, we have

$$\sin \theta = \frac{k}{m} \cdot \frac{y}{h}; \quad \sin \phi = \frac{k}{n} \cdot \frac{h-y}{h}.$$

$$\therefore \quad m \sin \theta + n \sin \phi = k,$$

which proves the construction.

The shape of the curve depends very much on the values of the constants m, n, k; that in the figure has been drawn for the equation $5 \sin \theta + 2 \sin \phi = 6$.

The sines of θ and ϕ are equal for the point C which is on the perpendicular to AB at its middle point, and the value of each is $\dfrac{k}{m+n}$. If through B a parallel to AC is drawn, the point at infinity on this line belongs to the locus. In the same way a parallel to BC drawn through A meets the curve at infinity. Only the portion of the locus at the upper side of AB is drawn.

The angles which satisfy the equation

$$m \sin \theta - n \sin \phi = k, \quad \dotfill (6)$$

where m, n, k are positive constants, can be deduced from the curve of Fig. 35 as in the analogous cases already explained.

A special and useful case of (6) occurs when $k = 0$, *i.e.*, when

$$m \sin \theta = n \sin \phi. \quad \dotfill (7)$$

Let A and B be any two fixed points and P a point whose dipolar angles, PAB and PBA, are θ and ϕ, respectively; then (7) gives $PA : PB = m : n$; hence since the base AB is given, the locus of P is a circle thus constructed: divide AB internally at O so that $AO : OB = m : n$, and externally at O' so that $AO' : O'B = m : n$; then the circle described on the line OO' as diameter is the locus of P. This is the well-known consequence of Euclid VI. 3. Of course the right line AB itself indefinitely produced both ways is part of the locus (7), because for all points on it $\sin \theta$ and $\sin \phi$ vanish.

To represent as dipolar angles all values of θ and ϕ satisfying the equation

$$m \tan \theta + n \tan \phi = k. \quad \dotfill (1)$$

On a right line take $AO = m$, $OB = n$; at O draw a perpendicular OH to AB, and take $OH = k$; join A to any point, C, on OH; take

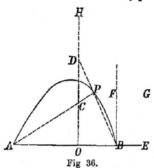

Fig 36.

$HD = OC$; draw AC and BD, intersecting in P; then P is a point on the required locus. For, $OC = AO \tan \theta$, $DO = OB \tan \phi$, $\therefore\ OH = AO \tan \theta + OB \tan \phi$, which is (8). In this way we trace out the locus APB.

The curve representing the angles which satisfy

$$m \tan \theta - n \tan \phi = k \quad\dots\dots\dots\dots\dots(9)$$

may be regarded as that shown above if we take the external angle PBE as ϕ; or if we wish to show θ and ϕ as both internal angles, we have merely to drop a perpendicular, PF, from P on BF (which is drawn at right angles to AB), and produce PF to G so that $PF = FG$; then the intersection of AP with BG gives a point on the curve (9), the angles θ, ϕ being PAB and GBA.

To represent as dipolar angles all the values of θ and ϕ satisfying the equation

$$m \sec \theta + n \sec \phi = k. \quad\dots\dots\dots\dots\dots(10)$$

In Fig. 36 take $AO = m$, $OB = n$, and at O erect a perpendicular, OH, to AB; draw AC from A to any point, C, on OH; with B as centre and a length equal to $k - AC$ as radius describe a circle cutting OH in D; then the point of intersection of AC and BD is a point on the locus. For if $CAO = \theta$, we have $AC = m \sec \theta$; and if $DBO = \phi$, we have $BD = n \sec \phi$; but $AC + BD = k$; therefore the angles CAO and DBO satisfy (10).

To represent as dipolar angles all values of θ and ϕ satisfying the equation

$$m \cot \theta + n \cot \phi = k. \quad\dots\dots\dots\dots\dots(11)$$

By letting $\theta = \frac{\pi}{2} - \theta'$ and $\phi = \frac{\pi}{2} - \phi'$, this becomes (8) in which θ' and ϕ' are the dipolar angles, while θ and ϕ are their complements. But if we wish to make θ and ϕ the angles PAB and PBA, we have a very simple representation of (11), thus:

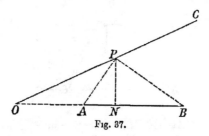

Fig. 37.

Let P be any position of the point such that $PAB = \theta$, $PBA = \phi$, and let PN be the perpendicular from P on AB. Then $\cot \theta = \frac{AN}{NP}$, $\cot \phi = \frac{BN}{NP}$; hence (11) becomes

$$m \cdot AN + n \cdot BN = k \cdot NP. \quad \text{...............}(12)$$

Suppose $m > n$; then this can be written

$$(m - n) AN + n \cdot AB = k \cdot NP,$$

or
$$\frac{n}{m-n} AB + AN = \frac{k}{m-n} \cdot NP. \text{...............}(13)$$

Measure AO along the line BA so that $AO = \frac{n}{m-n} AB$; that is, take O so that $BO : OA = m : n$, then (13) asserts that

$$\frac{ON}{NP} = \frac{k}{m-n}; \quad \text{.....................}(14)$$

and this shows that the angle POA is constant for all positions of P; in other words, the locus of P is a right line, OC, through O making $\cot^{-1} \frac{k}{m-n}$ with AB.

If m and n have opposite signs, the point O divides AB internally so that $AO : OB = n : m$ and the result (in both cases) is the familiar *cotangent formula* of Statics (see Minchin's *Statics*, Vol. I, Art. 36).

EXAMPLES.

1. Find graphically the values of θ and ϕ, less than 180°, which satisfy the equations

$$5 \tan \theta + 3 \tan \phi = 30, \dots\dots\dots\dots\dots\dots(1)$$

$$6 \cos \theta + 4 \cos \phi = 3. \dots\dots\dots\dots\dots (2)$$

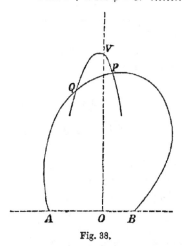

Fig. 38.

Take $AO = 5$, $BO = 3$, and construct the curve $AQPB$ given by the second equation, by describing about A as centre a circle of radius $\frac{2}{3} \cdot AB$, i.e., 16; and about B a circle of radius $\frac{4}{3} \cdot AB$, i.e., $10\frac{2}{3}$, and proceeding as in p. 52. Construct also the curve QVP representing the first equation.

These curves intersect at Q and P; and by means of a circular protractor we read

$$QAB = 78° 30'; \quad QBA = 63° 30', \dots\dots\dots\dots(\alpha)$$

$$PAB = 66°; \quad PBA = 81°. \dots\dots\dots\dots(\beta)$$

Taking the pair (α) we find the left-hand side of (1) to amount to 30·5928, and the left-hand side of (2) is 2·0810, which results show that the readings from the figure are fairly good. To obtain more accurate values of θ and ϕ, let $\theta = 78° 30' + x$ and $\phi = 63° 30' + y$, where x and y are small corrections in circular measure. Then $\tan \theta = \tan 78^\circ 30' + x \sec^2 78^\circ 30'$, very nearly, so that (1) becomes

$$30\,5928 + 5x \sec^2 78^\circ 30' + 3y \sec^2 63^\circ 30' = 30,$$

$$\therefore\ 125{\cdot}790x + 15{\cdot}069y = -{\cdot}593. \quad \dots\dots\dots(3)$$

In the same way, since $\cos(\theta + \Delta\theta) = \cos\theta - \sin\theta \,.\, \Delta\theta$, (2) becomes

$$4{\cdot}899x + 2\,685y = -{\cdot}019. \quad \dots\dots\dots\dots(4)$$

These equations (3) and (4) give $x = -{\cdot}004$, about, which is equivalent to $-13'45''$, so that the corrected value of θ is about $78^\circ 16'$. The value of y is $-{\cdot}007$. The second set of values (β) make the left-hand side of (1) equal to $30{\cdot}171$ and that of (2) equal to $3\,066$.

2. Find the values of θ and ϕ, less than 180°, which satisfy the equations

$$6\cos\theta + 4\cos\phi = 3, \quad \dots\dots\dots\dots\dots(1)$$

$$2\sin\theta - 3\sin\phi = 0. \quad \dots\ \dots\dots\dots\dots(2)$$

Employing the curve $AQPB$, Fig. 38, to represent (1), the distance AB being any whatever, construct the circle which represents (2). The diameter of this circle is $\frac{12}{5}AB$, and its centre is at the left of A at a distance $\frac{4}{5}AB$ from A. Drawing this circle, we find that it intersects $AQPB$ in a point above AB for which the values of θ and ϕ, measured by a protractor, are about

$$90^\circ \text{ and } 42^\circ 30'.$$

These make the left-hand sides of (1) and (2) equal to $2\,95$ and $0\,03$, nearly; and they can be corrected as above.

3. Find the values of θ and ϕ which satisfy the equations

$$6\cos\theta + 4\cos\phi = 3,$$

$$7\sin\theta - 3\sin\phi = 0.$$

The uncorrected values read with a protractor are

$$\theta = 20^\circ 30', \quad \phi = 126^\circ.$$

4. Find the values of θ and ϕ which satisfy

$$6\sin\theta + 4\sin\phi = 3,$$

$$7\cos\theta - 3\cos\phi = 0.$$

Let $\theta = 90^\circ - \theta'$, $\phi = 90^\circ - \phi'$; then these equations become those of the last example, and hence the uncorrected values of θ and ϕ are $69°\,30'$ and $-36°$, or if the latter is measured clockwise from the upper side of BA, $360°-36°$.

5. Find the values of θ and ϕ which satisfy

$$5\tan\theta + 3\tan\phi = 14, \quad\quad\quad\quad (1)$$

$$\sec\theta + 2\sec\phi = 6. \quad\quad\quad\quad (2)$$

Take a line AB, Fig. 39, and divide it at O so that $AO=5$, $BO=3$. Also divide it at O' into two segments such that $AO':O'B=1:2$; that is $AO'=\frac{1}{3}AB=2\frac{2}{3}$, and $O'B=5\frac{1}{3}$. Multiply (2) across by $\frac{8}{3}$, and it becomes

$$\tfrac{8}{3}\sec\theta + \tfrac{16}{3}\sec\phi = 16. \quad\quad\quad\quad (3)$$

At O' erect a perpendicular, $O'V'$, to AB, and construct a curve, $Q'PR'$, representing (3), as explained at p. 57. Construct also, using the perpendicular OV, the curve, QPR, representing (1), as explained at p. 57. These curves intersect in only one point, P, above AB, for which we find

$$\angle PAB = \theta = 60°\,30', \text{ and } \angle PBA = \phi = 60°.$$

These values make the left-hand side of (1) equal to $14\,033$, and that of (2) equal to $6\cdot031$.

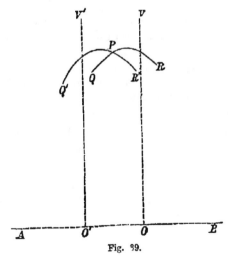

Fig. 39.

The student will observe that it is not necessary to trace the whole of each curve: we need to trace accurately only the parts in the neighbourhood of the point or points in which they intersect.

To avoid fractional parts of divisions in measuring AO', we have taken three sides of a square on squared paper to represent a unit length.

6. P is a point at a height of 5 feet above the surface of water; Q is a luminous point at a depth of 3 feet below the surface; M and N are the feet of the perpendiculars from P and Q, respectively, on the surface; the distance $MN = 10$ feet; find the ray of light emanating from Q which by refraction reaches P, the index of refraction being taken as $\frac{4}{3}$.

If R is the point in which the required ray from Q strikes the surface and θ, ϕ are the angles RPM, RQN, we have

$$5 \tan \theta + 3 \tan \phi = 10, \dots\dots\dots\dots\dots\dots(1)$$
$$3 \sin \theta - 4 \sin \phi = 0. \dots\dots\dots\dots \dots(2)$$

The problem leads therefore to the loci discussed in pages 57 and 56; and we find the readings to be $\theta = 57°$, $\phi = 39°$, which make the left-hand sides of (1) and (2) equal to 10·128 and − ·001, respectively.

The following problem leads also to two equations of the forms (1) and (2): AB and BC are two bars of weights P and Q freely jointed together at B; the first is moveable about a smooth horizontal axis fixed at A, while the end C of the second can move along a rough horizontal plane passing through A; given all necessary particulars, find the position of limiting equilibrium of the system.

7   Represent all values of θ and ϕ which satisfy the equation $m \tan \theta = n \tan \phi$, where m and n are given constants.

Take any right line AB; divide it at O so that

$$AO : OB = m : n;$$

at O draw a perpendicular to AB. If P is any point on this perpendicular, the lines PA and PB make the angles θ, ϕ with AB.

8. Solve, graphically, the equations

$$m \tan \theta = n \tan \phi,$$
$$a \sin \theta = b \sin \phi.$$

These angles determine the stationary positions of any two planets in their relative motion.

If S is the sun, E a planet distant r and P a planet distant R from S, θ and ϕ the acute angles made with EP by SE and SP, respectively, t and T the periodic times of E and P, the equations are

$$t \cdot \tan \theta = T \cdot \tan \phi,$$
$$r \cdot \sin \theta = R \cdot \sin \phi.$$

Hence the angles are given by the intersection of a right line and a circle.

9. If θ and ϕ are the base angles of a triangle, in which of the following cases will the vertical angle be least?—

$$\left. \begin{array}{l} 2 \tan \theta + 7 \tan \phi = 10 \\ 3 \sin \theta = 2 \sin \phi \end{array} \right\}, \quad \text{or} \quad \left. \begin{array}{l} 8 \tan \theta + 3 \tan \phi = 10 \\ 3 \sin \theta = 2 \sin \phi \end{array} \right\}.$$

In the second case, because then $\theta = 34°$, $\phi = 57°$; whereas in the first $\theta = 31° 30'$, $\phi = 51° 30'$.

This contains the answer to the question: the two legs of a double ladder are freely jointed together and have lengths 12 feet and 8 feet, their weights being proportional to their lengths. They rest on a rough horizontal plane for which the coefficient of friction is $\frac{1}{2}$. If they are gradually drawn apart, which will slip first? The longer.

DIPOLAR CO-ORDINATES.

Radii Vectores.

The position of a point P may, as already stated, be determined by the distances, PA and PB, of P from two fixed points, A, B. The simplest case occurs when the sum or difference of these distances is constant in all positions of P.

28. The Ellipse. Let A, B (Fig. 40) be two fixed points with a distance $2c$ between them, and let P be a point the sum of whose distances, r, r', from A and B is constant and equal to $2a$, where of course $a > c$; then P moves so that

$$r + r' = 2a \dots\dots\dots\dots\dots\dots(1).$$

Produce AB to C so that $AC = 2a$; about A as centre describe a series of circles of any radii; let PQP' be one of them; place the point of one leg of a pair of dividers at C and the point of the other leg at Q; with B as centre and the length CQ as radius describe a circle—or more simply with the dividers find the points

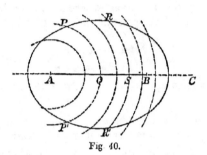

Fig 40.

P, P' in which this circle cuts PQP'; then P and P' are points on the ellipse. Similarly R, R', and all other points on the curve are found.

29. The Hyperbola. If P moves so that $PA - PB = 2a$, a constant, the locus is a hyperbola; and of course a must be less than c, since by Euclid I. 20 the difference between any two sides of a triangle is less than the third. Take, then,

$$r - r' = 2a. \qquad \dots\dots\dots\dots\dots\dots ..(2)$$

Measure $AC = 2a$; describe a series of circles round A as centre; let PQP' be one of them; with the length CQ as radius describe a circle round B as centre; if this intersects PQP' in P and P', these are points on the hyperbola, one branch of which is shown in Fig. 41. The other branch is similarly placed about A and it possesses the property that

$$r' - r = 2a. \qquad \dots\dots\dots\dots\dots\dots.(3)$$

Analytically the equations (1), (2), (3) of the ellipse and the hyperbola are the same; for, the expressions for r and r' in terms of the rectangular co-ordinates of P involve square roots which are got rid of by rationalizing the equations. Thus if AB is taken as axis of x and the origin is at its middle point, whether we rationalize (1), (2), or (3), we obtain the result

$$\frac{x^2}{a^2} + \frac{y^2}{a^2 - c^2} = 1.$$

For the ellipse $a^2 - c^2$ is positive and if it is put equal to b^2, we obtain $\frac{x^2}{a^2} + \frac{y^2}{b^2} = 1$; for the hyperbola $c^2 - a^2$ is positive, and if it is put equal to b^2, we obtain $\frac{x^2}{a^2} - \frac{y^2}{b^2} = 1$.

Analytically, then, the equation

$$mr + nr' = k \text{ includes } \pm mr \pm nr' = k;$$

for when the equation is wholly rationalized the difference of signs disappears.

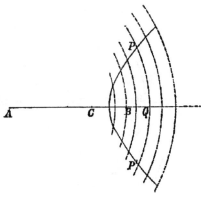

Fig. 41.

30. The Cartesian Oval. The curve whose equation in dipolar vectors is

$$mr + nr' = k, \quad \dots\dots\dots\dots\dots(1)$$

is called the *Cartesian Oval*. The ellipse and hyperbola are, of course, particular cases of this equation.

A rapid way of drawing the curve is as follows: take any two axes, Ox, Oy, and draw the right line whose equation with reference to them is

$$mx + ny = k; \quad \dots\dots\dots\dots\dots(2)$$

then taking any point, p, on this line, its co-ordinates being x and y, about A as centre describe a circle of radius x, and about B as centre a circle of radius y; the points, P, P', in which these circles intersect are points on the curve.

As before explained, the complete curve will correspond to the equations which we get by changing the signs of m and n in (1), so that points, p, on the auxiliary line (2) having negative co-ordinates are to be used in drawing the two circles round A and B.

As an example, let the equation be

$$5r \pm 2r' = 30. \quad \dots\dots\dots\dots\dots\dots(3)$$

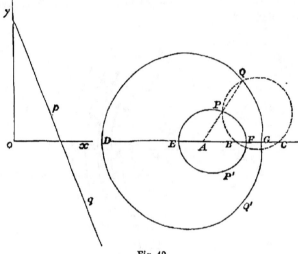

Fig. 42.

Taking axes Ox, Oy, the right line is

$$5x + 2y = 30,$$

and if we take points on this line with negative co-ordinates, we shall include the double sign in (3). The point p on the line determines the two points P, P' on the oval. When the point is taken so far up the line that $y - x < AB$, we get no real point on the oval. In the figure AB has been taken as 4 units. When p is taken so that $y - x = AB$, or $x - y = AB$, we get two coincident points on the oval. The curve consists of two ovals; and all points on the ovals are derived from points on the line pq thus: on Ox take a point H such that $OH = AB$; take also on Ox a point H' such that $OH' = -AB$; on Oy take also two points, K, K', such that $OK = AB$, $OK' = -AB$; then all points on pq

between the points in which it is met by $H'K$ and HK' give real points on the inner oval; and all points on pq included between those in which it is met by KH and $K'H'$ determine real points on the outer oval.

For points on the inner oval the equation is (1), while for points on the outer the equation is

$$mr - nr' = k. \quad \dots\dots\dots\dots\dots\dots(4)$$

Properties of the Ovals. Let the line AB meet the ovals in D, E, F, G, and denote AB by c. Then

$$mAF + n(AF - c) = k, \quad \therefore \ AF = \frac{k + cn}{m + n}, \text{ and } BF = \frac{k - cm}{m + n};$$

hence for the figure as drawn

$$k > cm. \quad \dots\dots\dots\dots\dots\dots(5)$$

Also $AE = \dfrac{k - cn}{m + n}$, $AD = \dfrac{k + cn}{m - n}$, $BG = \dfrac{k - cm}{m - n}$, and also

$$k > cn \quad \dots\dots\dots\dots\dots\dots(6)$$

Now we can prove that if any line through A meets the ovals in P and Q, the product

$$AP \cdot AQ \text{ is constant.}$$

For if $\angle QAB = \theta$, we have $BP^2 = r^2 + c^2 - 2cr \cos \theta$, and

$$BP = \frac{k - mr}{n} \text{ where } r = AP.$$

This gives

$$(m^2 - n^2) r^2 - 2(km - cn \cos \theta) r + k^2 - c^2 n^2 = 0,$$

the two roots of which for all values of $\cos \theta$ have the constant product $(k^2 - c^2 n^2)/(m^2 - n^2)$; and as this product is positive, the two values of r are AP and AQ.

We shall denote the distances of a point, P, on the inner oval from A and B by r_1 and r_2 respectively, and the distances of a point on the outer oval from A and B by R_1 and R_2, respectively. Hence

$$R_1 \cdot r_1 = \frac{k^2 - c^2 n^2}{m^2 - n^2}: \quad \dots\dots\dots\dots\dots(7)$$

We have the same kind of result for focal distances measured from B, with a certain difference. If ϕ is the angle which any line BP through B makes with AB, we have

$$r_1^2 = r_2^2 + c^2 - 2cr_2 \cos \phi;$$

5—2

or putting
$$r_1 = \frac{k - nr_2}{m}$$

$$(m^2 - n^2) r_2^2 + 2(kn - cm \cos \phi) r_2 - (k^2 - c^2m^2) = 0,$$

which shows that for all values of $\cos \phi$, the product of the values of r_2 is negative, by (6); and therefore the values of r_2 are BP and the production, BS, of PB backwards, i.e.,

$$R_2 \cdot r_2 = \frac{k^2 - c^2m^2}{m^2 - n^2}, \quad \dots \dots \dots \dots (8)$$

it being understood that R_2 and r_2 are always taken in opposite senses.

A third focus. We shall now show that there is a third focus, C.

Let a circle be described through P, Q, B; then whatever be the position of AQ, this circle cuts the line AB in a fixed point, C; for since $AB \cdot AC = AP \cdot AQ$, and this is constant, we have the result that AC is fixed. Denote AC by b; then

$$b = \frac{1}{c} \cdot \frac{k^2 - c^2n^2}{m^2 - n^2}. \quad \dots \dots \dots \dots (9)$$

We have now to show that the same kind of linear relation as (1) connects distances.

Since the quadrilateral $CBPQ$ is in a circle, the triangles APB and ACQ are similar; hence

$$\frac{AP}{AB} = \frac{CA}{AQ} \quad \text{and} \quad \frac{BP}{AB} = \frac{QC}{QA}.$$

Let $AQ = R_1$, $QC = R_3$, while $AP = r_1$, $BP = r_2$; then

$$r_1 = c \frac{b}{R_1}; \quad r_2 = c \frac{R_3}{R_1},$$

so that (1) becomes

$$kR_1 - cnR_3 = mbc, \quad \dots \dots \dots \dots (10)$$

showing that C is a third focus. We may easily conclude that if $PC = r_3$, this relation (10) for the outer oval implies the relation

$$kr_1 + cnr_3 = mbc \quad \dots \dots \dots \dots (11)$$

for the inner; and this can be proved from the similarity of the triangles QAB and CAP, thus:

$$\frac{r_2}{b} = \frac{R_2}{R_1}, \quad \therefore R_2 = \frac{R_1}{b} r_3; \quad \text{but } mR_1 - nR_2 = k, \quad \therefore mR_1 - n\frac{R_1}{b} r_3 = k,$$

and since $r_1R_1 = bc$, this gives (11).

From (1) and (11) we have $knr_2 - cmnr_3 = -(m^2bc - k^2)$, and if we denote BC by a, we have $a = \dfrac{k^2 - c^2m^2}{c(m^2 - n^2)}$, and this equation becomes

$$kr_2 - cmr_3 = -nac, \dots\dots\dots\dots \dots\dots(12)$$

for the inner oval, while for the outer the equation is found to be

$$kR_2 - cmR_3 = nac. \dots\dots\dots\dots\dots(13)$$

Analogous to the product relations (7) and (8), there is a product relation for the third focus. For if we use (12) and let ψ be the angle PCB we have for r_3 the equation

$$(k^2 - c^2m^2)\, r_3^2 + 2a\,(c^2mn - k^2\cos\psi) + a^2\,(k^2 - c^2n^2) = 0, \quad \dots(14)$$

the product of whose roots is constant and equal to ab. The difference between this and the cases for the foci A and B is that the two values of r_3 in (14) belong both to the same oval.

Hence we have the equations

$$R_1 . r_1 = bc, \dots\dots\dots\dots\dots (15)$$
$$R_2 . r_2 = ca, \dots\dots\dots\dots\dots(16)$$
$$r_3 . r_3' = R_3 . R_3' = ab, \dots\dots\dots\dots\dots(17)$$

where R_2 and r_2 are supposed to be measured in opposite senses and r_3, r_3' are the lengths cut off by the inner oval, and R_3, R_3' the lengths cut off by the outer, from any line drawn through C.

There is in addition to these three foci a triple focus with which we are not now concerned.

A Cartesian oval possesses a certain interest from the fact that it is the curve of accurate refraction of a ray of light from a given point in one medium to a given point in another. Thus, suppose that rays of light diverging from C in one medium are required to be refracted accurately to a point A in another, the second being the denser and the relative index of refraction being μ. If the boundary between the media consists of the surface generated by the revolution of the oval EPF round AC, the dipolar equation of the oval is $r_2 + \mu r_1 = \text{const.}$ This will be identical with (11) if

$$\mu = \frac{k}{cn}.$$

31. The Oval of Cassini. If A and B are any two fixed points, and P a variable point whose distances from A and B are r and r', the locus of P when

$$r . r' = a^2, \dots\dots\dots\dots\dots(1)$$

where a is a constant, is the oval of Cassini.

A simple way of constructing this curve is as follows: draw a right line DE (Fig. 43) of length $2a$; let O be its middle point;

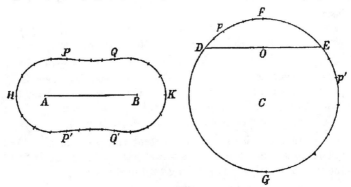

Fig. 43.

describe any circle through the points D and E; then if pOp' is any chord of this circle passing through O, we have $Op \cdot Op' = a^2$. But we may with advantage take OC perpendicular to DE and make $OC = \frac{1}{2}AB = c$, and take the circle with centre C. Then if we draw any chord pOp' of this circle through O, we may take $Op = r$ and $Op' = r'$ in (1); that is, about A describe a circle of radius Op and about B describe a circle of radius Op', and these circles will intersect in points P, P' on the required Cassinian oval. We may of course describe round B the circle of radius Op and round A that of radius Op', and we get Q, Q' on the oval.

With the circle chosen, if $FOCG$ is the chord perpendicular to DE, the points H, K of the oval correspond to F, G.

EXAMPLE.

1. There are two points, A, B, 20 metres apart; the product of the distances of a certain point P from A and B is 225 square metres, and the line AB subtends an angle of $40°$ at P; find the position of P.

A circle whose arc contains an angle of $40°$ has its centre on the line bisecting AB perpendicularly and at a distance of 11.92 from AB, Fig. 43. Constructing accurately the portion of the Cassinian oval $rr' = 225$ which is in the neighbourhood of the point of intersection, we find the readings to be

$$PA = 25\tfrac{3}{4}, \quad PB = 8\tfrac{3}{4}.$$

The angle PAB reads about $16° 30'$. Of course the values of PA and PB may be interchanged. Corrected values are obtained by assuming $r = 25\frac{3}{4} + x$, $r' = 8\frac{3}{4} + y$, where x and y are small. Then we have

$$(25\tfrac{3}{4} + x)(8\tfrac{3}{4} + y) = 225,$$

$$\therefore \quad 35x + 103y = -1·25. \quad \text{.................(1)}$$

We have also the equation $r^2 + r'^2 - 2rr' \cos 40° = 20^2$, which gives

$$103x + 35y = 10·19; \quad \text{.................(2)}$$

and these give $x = ·116$, $y = -·051$, so that the corrected values are

$$r = 25·866; \quad r' = 8·699.$$

MISCELLANEOUS METHODS.

32. The Lemniscate of Bernoulli. The polar equation of the lemniscate is

$$r^2 = a^2 \cos 2\theta. \quad \text{.....................(1)}$$

If the line from which θ is measured is taken as the major axis of a rectangular hyperbola, the equation of the hyperbola is

$$r'^2 \cos 2\theta = a^2, \quad \text{.....................(2)}$$

so that $rr' = a^2$, and the lemniscate is the inverse of the hyperbola with regard to its centre. In this way the lemniscate might be constructed easily, because by means of the *intercept property* (p. 24) a hyperbola is very rapidly drawn. The lemniscate is also the locus of the foot of the perpendicular from the centre of the rectangular hyperbola on the tangent to the hyperbola.

The following method of constructing the lemniscate is even more simple.

Let OA (Fig. 44) be the initial line and be equal to a; about A as centre with radius AO describe a circle; let Op be any line, making an angle θ with OA and meeting the circle in p; let pn be the perpendicular from p on OA; then $\angle pAn = 2\theta$, and $An = a \cos 2\theta$. Hence (1) can be written

$$r^2 = a \cdot An,$$

which shows that r is the y of a parabola whose vertex is A and latus rectum a; so that (without drawing the parabola by the method of p. 15) the simple construction is this: measure

$AD = \frac{1}{4}a$ along AO, measure $AE = \frac{1}{4}a$ perpendicular to AO, measure $AF = \frac{1}{4}a$ along An; draw the line DEL; let pn cut the

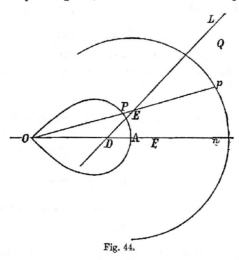

Fig. 44.

line in L; from F inflect the line FQ on npL equal to Ln; then measure OP equal to Qn, and we have a point P on the lemniscate.

(We see at once that

$$OP^2 = a^2 \cos 2\theta,$$

$\because Qn^2 = Ln^2 - Fn^2 = (a \cos 2\theta + \frac{1}{4}a)^2 - (a \cos 2\theta - \frac{1}{4}a)^2 = a^2 \cos 2\theta.$)

The tangents to the curve at O make angles of 45° with the diameter OA.

Only one half of the lemniscate is drawn: the other half lies to the left of O, which is the *node* of the curve. The *lemniscate* signifies literally the *ribbon* curve, the complete curve having a resemblance to a bow of ribbon, or a figure of 8.

Another simple construction of the lemniscate of Bernoulli is as follows: draw a right line OA of length a; on OA as diameter describe a circle; draw any line OR meeting the circle in R; with O as centre and OR as radius describe a circular arc; through A draw Ap parallel to OR, meeting this arc in p, from p draw pP perpendicular to OR; then $OP^2 = a^2 \cos^2 \theta - a^2 \sin^2 \theta = a^2 \cos 2\theta$, where θ is the angle ROA, so that P is on the lemniscate, and by varying OR we obtain all points on the lemniscate.

The General Lemniscate. The equation of the general lemniscate is

$$r^2 = a^2 \cos^2 \theta - b^2 \sin^2 \theta,$$

and this can be constructed by the last method described, thus: draw a line $OA = a$, and on this take $OB = b$; on OA as diameter describe a circle; through O draw OR meeting the circle in R; with O as centre and radius OR describe a circular arc; let a parallel through B to OR meet this arc in p; and from p draw pP perpendicular to OR; then P is on the lemniscate required. For $OP^2 = Op^2 - pP^2 = a^2 \cos^2 \theta - b^2 \sin^2 \theta.$

Other methods of describing these curves can be found by the student without difficulty.

EXAMPLES.

1. To construct a lemniscate of Bernoulli having a given point, O, for node and passing through two given points, B and C.

Let OA be the unknown diameter, of length a, and let it make the angle θ with OB.

Let $OB = b$, $OC = c$, and $\angle COB = \alpha$.

Then we have $b^2 = a^2 \cos 2\theta$, $c^2 = a^2 \cos 2(\theta + \alpha)$; therefore

$$\frac{b^2}{c^2} = \frac{\cos 2\theta}{\cos 2(\theta + \alpha)},$$

$$\therefore \tan 2\theta = \frac{b^2 \cos 2\alpha - c^2}{b^2 \sin 2\alpha},$$

which determines θ, and thence the value of a.

2. Let $OB = 8$ inches, $OC = 2$, and $\angle COB = 30°$, and find the lemniscate.

Result: the diameter makes an angle of $13° 24'$ with OB, and its length is $8\cdot46$ inches.

3. Let $OB = 8$ inches, $OC = 6$, $\angle COB = 30°$.

Result: the diameter lies between OB and OC, and is inclined to OB at about $2° 3' 45''$.

33. To find θ from the equation $a \sin 2(\theta - \alpha) = b \sin \theta$.

Let OA (Fig. 45) be the line from which θ is measured, and let $OA = b$; let OD be drawn making the angle $DOA = \alpha$; on OA

as diameter describe a circle, centre C; draw CD and produce it
to B so that $CB = a$, and on CB as diameter describe a circle.

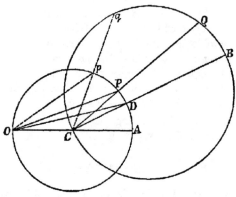

Fig. 45.

Let Op be a line making any angle, θ, with OA, p being on
the first circle; then $\angle pCD = 2\,(\theta - \alpha)$; produce Cp to meet the
second circle in q.

Now $Ap = b \sin \theta$, and $Bq = a \sin 2\,(\theta - \alpha)$; therefore if the
angle θ here satisfies the given equation, we should have

$$Ap = Bq.$$

This is not so in the figure: Bq is too large; and this shows
that the angle pOA is too large. We have to find by trial a point
P on the first circle such that if CP is produced to meet the
second circle in Q, we shall have $AP = BQ$. This relation is
satisfied in the figure, P being found very rapidly by trial; and
the required value of θ is therefore POA. Many problems in
Statics lead to the equation of this Article (Minchin's *Statics*,
Vol. I, pp. 169, 173).

Any equation of the form $b \cos\,(\theta + \alpha) = a \sin\,(2\theta + \beta)$ is
obviously reducible to the above form, as is also any equation
of the form

$$a \sin 2\theta + b \cos 2\theta + m \sin \theta + n \cos \theta = 0,$$

since $\qquad m \sin \theta + n \cos \theta = k \sin\,(\theta + \alpha),$

where $\qquad k = \sqrt{m^2 + n^2}$ and $\tan \alpha = \dfrac{n}{m}.$

Although the above shows very readily the approximate value of θ that satisfies the given equation, the following is more in accordance with our general method—which consists in constructing two loci whose points of intersection determine the unknown angle. Thus, to find ϕ from the equation

$$a \sin (\phi - \alpha) = b \sin 2\phi,$$

construct the curves, with O as origin and OA as initial line from which ϕ is measured,

$$r = \frac{b}{\sin (\phi - \alpha)}, \quad \dots \dots \dots (\alpha)$$

$$r = \frac{a}{\sin 2\phi}. \quad \dots \dots \dots (\beta)$$

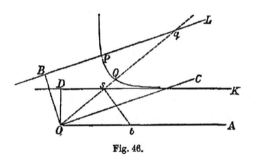

Fig. 46.

The curve (α) is a right line BL (Fig. 46) constructed thus: draw OC making the angle $COA = \alpha$; draw OB, equal to b, perpendicular to OC; at B draw the line BL parallel to OC. The curve (β) is thus constructed: draw OD, equal to $\frac{1}{2}a$, perpendicular to OA; draw the line DK parallel to OA; draw any line Oq cutting DK in s, the angle qOA being ϕ; at s draw st perpendicular to Oq; then $Ot = \dfrac{a}{2 \sin \phi \cos \phi}$, so that if we take $OQ = Ot$, the locus of Q is the curve (β).

A portion of the curve is shown in the figure, and the point P in which it cuts the line BL is that which determines the value, POA, of ϕ which satisfies the given equation.

EXAMPLES.

1.   To find θ from the equation

$$\sin^2 \theta \sin (\theta + \alpha) = k,$$

where α and k are given.

With pole O, Fig. 47, and initial line from which θ is measured, OA, construct the curves

$$r = \frac{k}{\sin (\theta + \alpha)}, \quad \cdots\cdots\cdots\cdots\cdots\cdots \quad (\alpha)$$

$$r = \sin^2 \theta. \quad \cdots\cdots \cdots\cdots\cdots\cdots\cdots\cdots (\beta)$$

To construct the first, which is a right line, draw OC making $\angle COA = \alpha$; at O draw a perpendicular to OC of length k and at the end of this draw a line QPR parallel to OC. To construct (β), about O as centre and with radius unity describe a circle; draw any line Op meeting the circle in p; draw OD at right angles to OA ; let n be the foot of the perpendicular from p on OD, and let r be the foot of the perpendicular from n on Op Then if $pOA = \theta$, we have $On = \sin\theta$ and $Or = \sin^2 \theta$.   The locus of r is a curve of which only the upper half is shown: the complete curve is a figure of 8.

This curve cuts the line QPR in the points Q and P, the polar angles, QOA and POA, of which are the required values of θ.

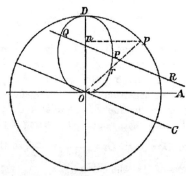

Fig 47.

2.   In the same way solve the equation $\sin^2 \theta \cos (\theta + \alpha) = k$.

3.   Solve graphically the equation $\sin^2 \theta (5 \sin \theta + 2 \cos \theta) = 4$.

The angle AOC is $\tan^{-1}\frac{2}{5}$, so that OC can be easily drawn on squared paper. The equation then becomes $\sin^2\theta \sin(\theta+\alpha) = 743$; k is therefore ·743. If the divisions of the squared paper are very small, 20 or 30 of them (or even more) can be conveniently taken to represent OA.

The value of the angle COP as read with a protractor is about $60°40'$; and when this is substituted in the given equation it makes the right-hand side equal to 4·057. This value of θ can then be corrected as explained in several other examples.

The second value, QOA, reads as 105°, and this makes the right-hand side equal to 4·023.

4 Solve the equation $\sin^2\theta(5\sin\theta - 2\cos\theta) = ·7$.

Result: the uncorrected values as read from the figure with a protractor are—

$\theta = 40°$, which makes the right-hand side equal to ·695.

$\theta = 155°$, which makes the right-hand side equal to ·701.

5. Show how to solve the equation
$$\sin^n\theta(a\sin\theta + b\cos\theta) = k,$$
where a, b, k are given quantities, and n is an integer.

[Another way of solving the equation
$$\sin^2\theta(a\sin\theta + b\cos\theta) = k,$$
suggested by Mr Alfred Lodge, is this: draw a line $OB = b$, and at right angles to it take $OA = a$; describe a circle through B, O, and A; if any line, OR, drawn through O meets the circle in R and makes an angle θ with OB, we have
$$OR = a\sin\theta + b\cos\theta.$$

If then from R we drop a perpendicular Rp on OA, and from p a perpendicular pP on OR, it is clear that
$$OP = \sin^2\theta(a\sin\theta + b\cos\theta).$$

Tracing the locus of P, we obtain an oval like $OPDQ$ in Fig. 47; but its axis of symmetry is inclined to OA. The points of intersection of this curve with the circle of radius k described about O as centre give the values of θ. This curve is, however, not so readily traced as that in Fig. 47.]

6. Show how to solve the equation $\sin^4\theta = k\sin(\theta-\alpha)$, where k and α are given constants.

7. Construct the curve whose equation is $y = \dfrac{\sqrt{x^2 + a^2} + a}{\sqrt{x^2 + b^2} + b}$,

where a and b are given constants.

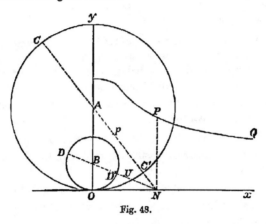

Fig. 48.

Take OA on the axis of y (Fig. 48) equal to a and describe a circle with A as centre; take $OB = b$, and describe a circle with B as centre. Let ON be any value of x; then drawing NA to meet the first circle in C, we have $NC = \sqrt{x^2 + a^2} + a$. Similarly, drawing NB to meet the second circle in D, we have $ND = \sqrt{x^2 + b^2} + b$. Hence the y of the point on the curve sought is $\dfrac{NC}{ND}$. To construct this take a unit length, NU, along NB and from U draw a parallel, Up, to DC; then

$$y = \frac{NC}{ND} = \frac{Np}{1}, \quad \therefore \ y = Np;$$

on the ordinate NP drawn at N measure $NP = Np$, and we have the point P on the required curve. Repeating this operation for all positions of N along Ox, we have the whole curve required. There is a similar portion of the curve (not shown) at the left-hand side of Oy, corresponding to negative values of x.

Observe that if the given equation is cleared of radicals, it will represent a curve of the 8th degree corresponding to any one of the relations

$$y = \frac{\pm\sqrt{x^2 + a^2} + a}{\pm\sqrt{x^2 + b^2} + b},$$

the differences of signs all disappearing in the process of rationalization.

These various signs correspond to the points C, C', D, D' in which the lines NA and NB meet the circles.

Thus, for example, a value of y which would be included in the rationalized result is $-\dfrac{NC}{ND'}$; and so on.

Unless a and b are very unequal, the curve does not differ much from a right line parallel to Ox.

Show how to solve the equation

$$e^{\frac{k}{x}} = \frac{\sqrt{x^2 + a^2} + a}{\sqrt{x^2 + b^2} + b}.$$

(This equation arises in the following problem: the ends of a heavy uniform chain, or wire rope, are fastened at two points in the same horizontal line; if a load is suspended from the lowest point of the catenary, the chain or rope forms two distinct catenaries starting to the right and left of the point of suspension of the load; calculate the new figure. Minchin's *Statics*, Vol. I, p. 399, fifth ed.)

As a numerical example, take $a = 45$, $b = 20$, $k = 10$, and a construction will give $x = 13\frac{1}{3}$, q.p. In constructing, it will be well to replace x by $5z$.

8. Construct the curve $y = x\,\dfrac{a + bx^2}{c + x^2}$; and hence show how to solve the equation

$$x\,\frac{a + bx^2}{c + x^2} = \tan^{-1}x. \quad\ldots\ldots\ldots\ldots\ldots\ldots(\alpha)$$

(This equation determines the figure of equilibrium of a rotating self-attracting spheroid.)

The given value of y can be written $y = bx + (a - bc)\,\dfrac{x}{c + x^2}$, so that the ordinate is the sum of the ordinates of a right line $y_1 = bx$ and the curve $y_2 = (a - bc)\,\dfrac{x}{c + x^2}$.

To construct y_2 let $x = \sqrt{c}\,\cot\theta$; then

$$y_2 = \frac{a - bc}{\sqrt{c}}\sin\theta\cos\theta.$$

On Oy, Fig. 49, take $OK = \sqrt{c}$ and draw the line Kp parallel to Ox; on Ox take $OH = \dfrac{a - bc}{\sqrt{c}}$, and on OH as diameter describe

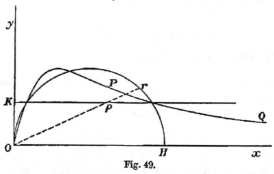

Fig. 49.

a circle; take any point, p, on Kp, and draw Opr meeting the circle in r; through r draw a parallel rP to Ox meeting the ordinate of p in P; then P is a point on the curve

$$y_2 = (a - bc)\frac{x}{c + x^2}.$$

For if the angle $pOH = \theta$, and x is the abscissa of p,

$$x = \sqrt{c}\cot\theta; \quad \text{and} \quad Or = \frac{a - bc}{\sqrt{c}}\cos\theta,$$

and the ordinate of r is $Or\sin\theta$, $i.e.$

$$\frac{a - bc}{\sqrt{c}}\sin\theta\cos\theta, \quad \text{or } y_2.$$

Drawing, then, the right line $y_1 = bx$ through O, the curve $y = x\dfrac{a + bx^2}{c + x^2}$ has its ordinate equal to the sum, $y_1 + y_2$, of the ordinates of the right line and the curve PQ corresponding to the same abscissa.

The intersections of this resultant curve and the curve $y = \tan^{-1}x$ determine the roots of (a).

9. Show how to solve the equations:

(1) $\tan x = x$,   (2) $\tan x = 2x$,

(3) $\tan x = \dfrac{2x}{2 - x^2}$,   (4) $\tan x = \dfrac{3x}{3 - 2x^2}$,

which occur in connection with Bessel functions. (Use hyperbolas in the last two.)

CHAPTER IV.

PROJECTION.

I. Construction of the Projections of Plane Figures.

34. Centre of Projection, Axis of Projection. Let there be a plane figure consisting of any number of points $A, B, C, \ldots$ straight lines $a, b, c, \ldots$ and curves $\sigma, \ldots$ lying in a plane π, and let a point S be taken outside the plane, and from S straight lines be drawn to every point of the figure in the plane π. These straight lines (produced if necessary) will meet a second plane π' in points forming a figure which is called the *projection* of the figure in the plane π.

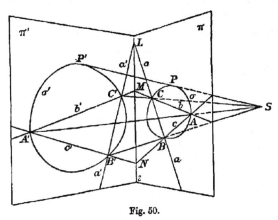

Fig. 50.

The point S is called the *centre of projection* or *perspective*, and s the line of intersection of the planes π and π' is called the *axis of projection* or *perspective*.

It is clear that the figure in either plane may be regarded as the projection of the other and such figures are said to *correspond*. Thus A and A' the projection of A are corresponding points, a and a' corresponding lines, σ and σ' corresponding curves.

35. The following theorems are obvious:

A point projects into a point.

A straight line projects into a straight line.

The straight line joining two points projects into the straight line joining the projections of the points.

Any number of points of a curve lying upon a straight line project into the same number of points of the projected curve lying upon a straight line.

A tangent to a curve projects into a tangent to the projected curve.

The number of tangents which can be drawn through a given point to a curve is unaltered by projection.

For example, a circle projects into a curve such that only two points lie upon a straight line, and only two tangents can be drawn to it from any given point.

Every point upon the axis of projection projects into itself.

Corresponding lines intersect upon the axis of projection.

36. Points and Lines at Infinity. Vanishing Points and Lines.

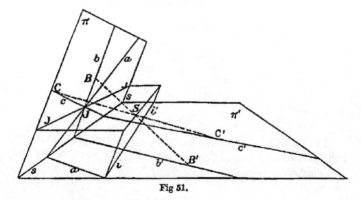

Fig 51.

If through the centre of projection S straight lines be drawn to the points lying at an infinite distance upon the plane π, these straight lines will lie in a plane through S parallel to π. The intersection of this plane with the plane π' will be a straight line i' parallel to s the axis of projection, for any two parallel planes are cut by a third plane in parallel lines. Since in general a straight line is the projection of a straight line, for the sake of continuity we regard i' as the projection of a straight line i which contains all the points at infinity upon the plane π; and i' is called the *vanishing line* of the plane π'.

In like manner the points at infinity upon the plane π' are to be regarded as lying upon a straight line j' which projects into the vanishing line j upon the plane π.

Since two planes intersect in one straight line only, there can be only one vanishing line in a plane.

If any number of straight lines $a, b, c, \ldots$ intersect in a point J upon the vanishing line j, their projections $a', b', c', \ldots$ intersect in a point J' upon the line at infinity j'. Hence $a', b', c', \ldots$ will be parallel. Conversely if $a, b, c, \ldots$ are parallel lines they will project into lines $a', b', c', \ldots$ intersecting upon the vanishing line i'.

37. Conical, Parallel and Orthogonal Projections.

When we project from one plane to another, the centre of projection S being at a finite distance, the projection is designated *conical*. In this form of projection the ratios of segments of lines will in general be altered, likewise the magnitudes of angles.

If however s, the axis of projection, be at infinity, so that the planes π and π' are parallel, corresponding lines in the original and projected figures will be parallel, and therefore the figures will be similar. Corresponding angles will be unaltered in magnitude, and all linear dimensions will be altered in the same ratio.

In the case when the centre of projection S is at infinity all lines joining corresponding points are parallel, and the projection is designated *parallel*.

6—2

If in addition all the projecting lines are at right angles to the plane of projection π', the projection is designated *orthogonal*.

In *parallel projection* parallel lines are projected into parallel lines, the ratios of the segments of parallel lines are altered in the same ratio, but angles are altered in magnitude.

Both vanishing lines are at infinity when either S or s are at infinity.

In Conical Projection we may consider that we are dealing with sections of a pyramid or cone, and in Parallel Projection with sections of a prism or cylinder.

38. *Any straight line can be projected to infinity and at the same time any two angles into two given angles.*

In order to project a given line j in the plane π to infinity with any centre of projection S, all that is necessary is to select the plane of projection π', so that it is parallel to the plane through S and j. In this way j becomes the vanishing line of the plane π.

We shall now prove that if the sides of an angle APB meet the vanishing line in the points A, B, APB projects into an angle equal to ASB.

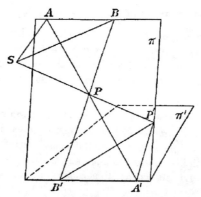

Fig. 52.

Let AP, BP meet the plane π' which is parallel to the plane ASB, in A' and B', and let P' be the projection of P. Then the plane $SAA'P'$ intersects the parallel planes ASB and π' in parallel lines SA and $P'A'$. Similarly the lines SB and $P'B'$ are parallel. Hence the angle $A'P'B'$ is equal to the angle ASB, and if ASB is given in magnitude, the point S may be taken anywhere upon an arc of a segment of a circle described upon AB as chord and containing the given angle.

If the sides of a second angle CQD intersect the vanishing line in C and D, this angle may in like manner be projected into an angle of given magnitude by taking the vertex of projection S upon an arc of a segment of a circle described upon CD as chord and containing the given angle.

The arcs described upon AB and CD will intersect in a real or imaginary point. The point will be real when the segments AB and CD overlap, but may be imaginary when they do not.

It should be noted that the plane containing S and the vanishing line is quite arbitrary, but π' must be parallel to it.

39. Theorem of Desargues. *If two triangles ABC, $A'B'C'$ be placed so that the lines AA', BB', CC' joining pairs of corresponding points are concurrent in a point S, then L, M, N the points of intersections of corresponding lines $BC, B'C'$; $CA, C'A'$; $AB, A'B'$, lie upon a straight line s.*

First (Fig. 50) suppose the triangles ABC, $A'B'C'$ to lie in different planes π and π'. Then S is the centre of projection of the triangles, and a pair of corresponding lines such as $BC, B'C'$ will meet the line of intersection of the planes π and π' in the same point L, namely where the plane $SABA'B'$ is met by this line. Therefore the three points of intersection of corresponding sides lie upon this line which is the axis of projection.

Next suppose the triangles ABC, $A'B'C'$ to lie in the same plane π. With any centre of projection S project the triangles on to a plane π' so that the line MN is projected to infinity. Let $A_1B_1C_1$, $A_1'B_1'C_1'$ be the projections. Then since the projections of M and N are at infinity C_1A_1 is parallel to $C_1'A_1'$ and A_1B_1 to $A_1'B_1'$. Therefore the triangles $A_1B_1C_1$, $A_1'B_1'C_1'$ have two pairs of sides parallel and hence the remaining pair must also be parallel, in other words the projection of L is also at infinity. Therefore L must lie upon the straight line MN.

40. The Converse Theorem is also true.

If two triangles ABC, A'B'C' have the points of intersection of corresponding sides collinear, then the lines joining corresponding points are concurrent.

First suppose the triangles ABC, $A'B'C'$ to lie in different planes π and π'. L, M, N the points of intersection of corresponding sides must lie upon s the line of intersection of the planes. Then the pairs of sides determine three planes $BCB'C'$, $CAC'A'$, $ABA'B'$ which intersect in a point S, and SAA', SBB', SCC' are the lines of intersection of the planes.

Next suppose the triangles ABC, $A'B'C'$ to lie in the same plane π. Then as before we may project the line LMN to infinity and therefore the triangles into triangles whose corresponding sides are parallel. Hence the triangles are similar and the lines joining corresponding points are concurrent; and therefore the lines AA', BB', CC' must also be concurrent.

41. Generalising the above result we say that figures in the same or different planes are in perspective, when they are so related that the lines joining corresponding points are concurrent, and the points of intersection of corresponding sides are collinear.

If two figures σ and σ' in different planes π and π' are in perspective, they will remain in perspective when the plane π' is rotated about the axis of perspective so as to come into coincidence with the plane π.

Since the figures are in perspective corresponding lines will always meet upon the axis of perspective, and therefore even when the planes are coincident the lines joining corresponding points will be concurrent.

42. *When the plane π' is rotated about the axis of perspective s, the centre of perspective S describes a circle in a plane at right angles to s having its centre upon the vanishing line j.*

Through S draw a plane at right angles to s, and let it cut s in O and the vanishing lines i' and j in I' and J. Then since SI', SJ are parallel to JO, $I'O$, $SI'JO$ is a parallelogram, and since JO, $I'O$ are of constant length, so likewise are SI', SJ. Therefore when π' is turned about s, I' and S will describe circles in the plane $SI'JO$ about the points O and J as centres respectively.

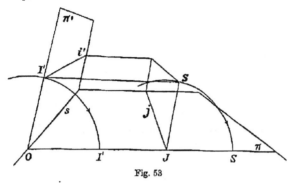

Fig. 53

The operation of turning one plane into coincidence with another is designated *rabatting* the plane.

43. We have seen that the points $SOJI'$ always lie in a plane perpendicular to s; hence when the plane π' is rabatted on to the plane π, these points will lie on a straight line at right angles to s.

It is obvious that J and I' will lie on the same or opposite sides of O according to the direction in which π' is turned about s. In all cases however $JO = SI'$ and are measured in the same direction, hence whenever three of the points are known the remaining one can be immediately determined.

44. We now proceed to consider the following fundamental construction.

Given the centre of projection S, the axis of projection s, and a pair of corresponding points A and A' rabatted into one plane, to determine the point B' corresponding to a given point B.

Since AA', BB' are pairs of corresponding points, SAA', SBB' must be straight lines, and AB and $A'B'$ must intersect upon s. Hence we produce AB to cut s in L, join $A'L$ and SB, and B' is the point of intersection of these two last lines.

If A is a point upon the vanishing line j, A' is at infinity in the direction SA. Therefore when L is determined as above LA' is to be drawn from L parallel to SA. It thus appears that we can determine any number of corresponding points when the centre and axis of projection and one vanishing line are given.

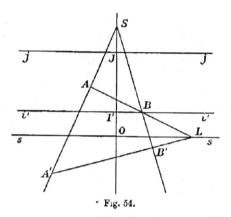

- Fig. 54.

45. In the same manner we solve the following problem.

Given the centre of projection S, the axis of projection s, and a pair of corresponding lines a and a' rabatted into one plane, to determine the line b' corresponding to a given line b.

Since *aa'*, *bb'* are pairs of corresponding lines, their points of intersection must lie upon *s*; also if *a*, *b* intersect at *P*, and *a'*, *b'* at *P'*, *P* and *P'* are corresponding points, and therefore *SPP'* is a straight line. Hence *P'* is determined by the intersection of *a'* and *SP*, and *b'* passes through *P'* and the intersection of *b* and *s*.

46 Construction of rabatted centre of Projection.

In constructing the projection of a figure we have first to determine the position of the centre of projection when rabatted into the plane of the figure.

The position of the centre of projection will usually be given in terms of its vertical distance above the plane of the figure and the distance from the axis of projection of the foot of the perpendicular dropped from it upon this plane. The angle between the plane of the figure and the plane of projection will also be given.

Let s be the axis of projection, N the foot of the perpendicular dropped from the centre of projection upon the plane of the figure.

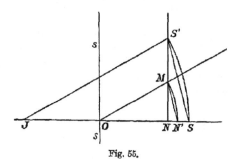

Fig. 55.

Draw NO at right angles to s, then S the rabatted centre of projection will lie upon NO.

Through O draw OM making the angle NOM equal to the angle between the planes, so that ON and OM represent sections of the planes π and π' by the perpendicular plane through S. Draw a line through N at right angles to ON and on it mark S' the position of the centre of projection. Through S' draw $S'J$, $S'I'$ parallel to OM and ON respectively; J and I' fix the positions of the vanishing lines.

With J as centre and radius JS' describe a circle; it will cut ON in S the position of the rabatted centre.

It frequently happens that J is at an inconveniently great distance from s. In this case we may substitute the following construction, and indeed it may preferably be used in every case.

If M is the point where $S'N$ meets the plane π', with O as centre and OM as radius describe a circle cutting ON in N'. Then MN' will be parallel to $S'S$ as determined by the former method, and hence S is found by drawing $S'S$ parallel to MN'.

Incidentally we have found the point N' corresponding to the point N, and hence since the rabatted positions of the centre of perspective, the axis of perspective and a pair of corresponding points are known, the positions of all other points may be determined.

47. Axis of Projection at Infinity. When the axis is at infinity, S will coincide with N the foot of the perpendicular from S' Also if AA' be a pair of corresponding points the ratio of SA' to SA will be equal to the ratio of $S'M$ to $S'N$.

48. Centre of Projection at Infinity. In this case all the projecting lines are parallel. Their direction will be determined by the angle they make with the plane of the figure π, and the angle made by their orthogonal projections upon this plane with the axis of perspective.

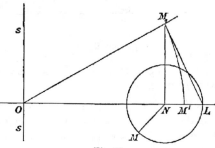

Fig. 56.

To find a pair of corresponding points we make the following construction. From any point O in the axis of projection, draw ON at right angles to the axis. Through O draw OM_1 making the angle NOM_1 equal to the angle between the planes π and π'. Draw M_1N at right angles to ON, and M_1L making the angle M_1LN equal to the angle between the projecting lines and the plane π. From N draw NM equal to NL in the direction of the orthogonal projections of the projecting lines upon the plane π. Lastly with O as centre and OM_1 as radius describe a circle cutting the line ON in M', then M and M' are a pair of corresponding points.

That this is the case may be at once seen by supposing the triangle NOM_1 turned round ON at right angles to the rest of the plane. It is then obvious that M_1M is a projecting line.

We proceed to illustrate the foregoing principles by applying them to the solution of some examples.

49 *To project a given quadrilateral ABCD into a square.*

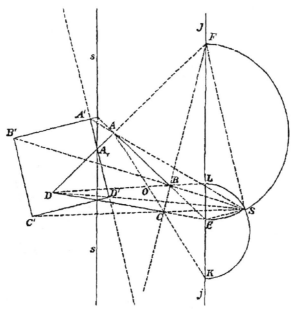

Fig. 57.

Let the sides AB, DC intersect in E, and the sides AD, BC in F. Then if EF is projected to infinity, the quadrilateral will be projected into a parallelogram. If in addition the angle FAE is projected into a right angle, the parallelogram will be a rectangle, and the rectangle will be a square if the angle COD between the diagonals is projected into a right angle.

Hence we have to project the line EF to infinity and at the same time the angles FAE, COD into right angles. Let AC and BD meet EF in K and L respectively. Upon EF and KL as diameters describe semi-circles intersecting in S. We take S as the centre of projection rabatted into the plane of the figure, EF is the vanishing line j, and we take any line s parallel to EF as the axis of perspective.

The projection of F lies at infinity upon SF. To find the
projection of A, let AF meet s in A_1, draw a line through A_1
parallel to SF and let SA meet this line in A', then A' is the
projection of A.

In the same manner the projections of the other points BCD
may be found.

50   *To construct the section of a right circular cone of height
10 inches standing upon a base of radius 3 inches made by a plane
inclined at an angle of 30° to the base, the line of intersection of the
planes being a tangent to the base.*

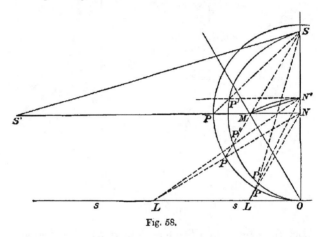

Fig. 58.

Draw a circle centre N of radius 3 inches. Take any point O
on it and draw the tangent at O. We take this tangent as the
axis of projection s. Through O draw a line making an angle of
30° with ON, and through N draw a line at right angles to ON
cutting the former line in M. Produce NM to S' a distance of
10 inches.

Take N' on ON so that $ON' = OM$ and draw $S'S$ parallel to
MN' meeting ON in S.

Then S is the rabatted centre of projection and NN' a pair of
corresponding points.

If P be any point on the circle and if PN intersect s in L,
then P' the point corresponding to P is the intersection of SP

and LN'. In this manner any number of points may be determined.

It is known however that the projected curve is a conic section, and a conic can be drawn when five points are known. Hence five points will be sufficient to determine the form of the projected curve.

51. *To construct the section of an oblique prism standing upon a regular hexagonal base made by a plane passing through one side of the base and inclined to it at an angle of 20°. The edges of the prism make an angle of 60° with the plane of the base, and their orthogonal projections are inclined at an angle of 50° to the axis of projection. The length of a side of the base is 2 inches.*

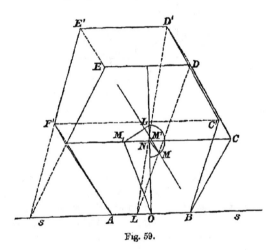

Fig. 59.

Construct a regular hexagon $ABCDEF$ whose sides are 2 inches long. Take AB as the axis of projection.

From O the middle point of AB, draw ON at right angles to AB and OM_1 making an angle of 20° with ON.

M_1 being any point on the line draw M_1N at right angles to ON, and also M_1L so that the angle $M_1LN = 60°$. From N draw NM equal to LN and making an angle of 40° with NO. Mark off on ON, OM' equal to OM_1, then M and M' are corresponding points.

To find the point D' corresponding to D, let MD intersect s in L; then D' is the point of intersection of LM' and a line through D parallel to MM'.

The projections of the other angular points may be determined in like manner or by making use of D and D'.

52. *To construct a triangle, ABC, Fig. 60, whose vertices shall lie on three concurrent lines, OA, OB, OC, and each of whose sides shall pass through a given point, P for one, Q for the second, and R for the third.*

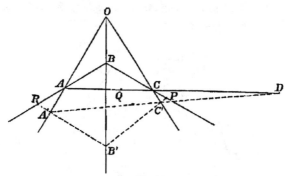

Fig. 60.

Draw any triangle, $A'B'C'$, satisfying all the conditions but one; that is, take any point, B', on OB, and join B' to R and to P; let $B'R$ meet OA in A' and $B'P$ meet OC in C'. Now consider the two triangles ABC and $A'B'C'$. They are in perspective; therefore the points of intersection, R, P, D, of corresponding sides lie in a right line; that is to say, the point D in which the base AC of the required triangle meets the line $A'C'$ is obtained by drawing the line RP and taking its intersection with $A'C'$. Hence the required base AC now passes through two known points, Q and D. Therefore joining D to Q we have AC; and finally joining A to R and C to P, we have the required triangle, ABC.

This construction is of extremely frequent occurrence in statical problems which deal with lines of resistance between bar and bar in a jointed framework.

Of course the lines AO, BO, CO may be parallel. For example, supposing a double ladder, ABC, consisting of two legs AB and BC freely jointed at B to be placed with the ends A, C on the ground; it is required to determine the lines of reaction at A, B, C. Let G be the centre of gravity of AB; let G' be the centre of gravity of BC; let G'' be the centre of gravity of the whole ladder; then the three vertical lines through G, G', and G'' are three given concurrent lines, and the points A, B, C the three given points which, as in the above problem, are to determine the triangle formed by the lines of resistance.

53. Projections of a Circle. The projections of a circle fall into three classes depending upon the nature of the intersections of the circle with the vanishing line of the plane.

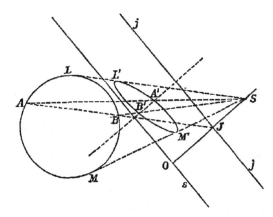

Fig. 61.

When the vanishing line does not cut the circle (Fig. 61) the projection is a closed curve called an *Ellipse*.

When the vanishing line touches the circle (Fig. 62) the projection is an open curve called a *Parabola*. If the point T is the point of contact of the vanishing line, ST is the direction of the points at infinity upon the curve. The parabola then is characterised by having the line at infinity as a tangent.

When the vanishing line cuts the circle in two distinct points
(Fig. 63) the projection is an open curve of two branches called
a *Hyperbola*.

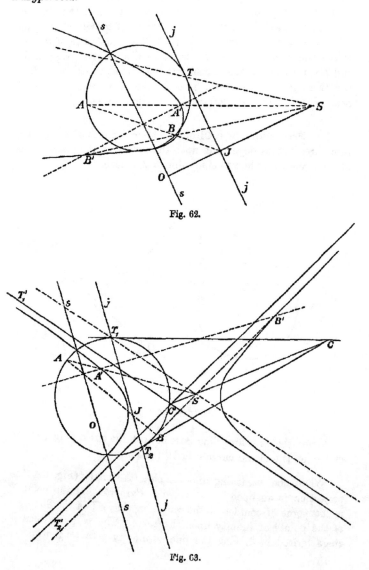

Fig. 62.

Fig. 63.

The tangents CT_1, CT_2 to the circle at the points where it is cut by the vanishing line project into tangents $C'T_1'$, $C'T_2'$ to the Hyperbola, the points of contact being at infinity. These tangents are called *Asymptotes*. Their directions are parallel to those of ST_1, ST_2.

II. Cross-Ratios.

54. All properties of a plane figure depending upon the collinearity of points or the concurrence of lines in the figure are unaltered by projection. On the other hand no simple relation exists between the magnitudes of corresponding angles or the lengths of corresponding segments of lines in the original figure and its projection. Bearing in mind however the fact that to any point in a figure corresponds one point and one only in its projection, it is possible to discover certain relations between lengths of segments of lines and the magnitudes of angles which remained unchanged by projection.

55. Segments of Lines. Let AB be any two points upon the straight line AB, then the portion of the line contained between the points is called the *segment AB*.

We find it desirable to associate with a segment the idea not only of *magnitude* but also of *direction* or *sense*. In this way AB is to be regarded as indicating a step from one point A of the line to another B of given magnitude and in one of the two possible directions of motion along the straight line. Hence AB and BA are segments equal in magnitude but opposite in sense and we may write

$$AB + BA = 0 \text{ or } AB = -BA.$$

If C be any third point on the line it follows at once that

$$AB + BC = AC \text{ and } AB + BC + CA = 0$$

whatever be the position of C relative to A and B.

It is clear then that we may use the algebraical signs $+$ and $-$ to distinguish the opposite directions of measurement along a straight line.

56. Ratio of Segments. If AB be any two points upon a straight line and P any other point, then the segment AB is said to be divided by P in the ratio $AP : PB$.

M. D.

The sign of this ratio is positive so long as AP and PB are measured in the same direction, that is so long as P lies between A and B. The sign is negative when P lies on any part of the line outside the segment AB. Supposing A to be to the left of B, it is clear that the ratio $AP \cdot PB$ increases algebraically from -1 to 0 as P comes from an infinite distance to the left up to A. The value increases from 0 to $+\infty$ as P moves from A to B. On passing through B the sign changes and as P moves to an infinite distance to the right the value increases from $-\infty$ to -1. Hence it follows that to a given value of the ratio corresponds one and only one position of P on the line AB.

Two values of the ratio equal in magnitude and opposite in sign are sometimes distinguished by saying that the corresponding positions of P divide AB internally and externally in the same ratio

57.   Problem.   *To divide a segment in a given ratio.*

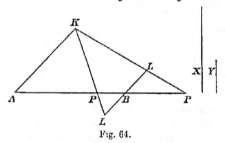

Fig. 64.

Let the given ratio be equal to that of two given lines X and Y, and let AB be the segment to be divided.

From A in any direction draw a straight line AK equal to X; and from B draw BL parallel to AK, in the same direction as AK if the given ratio is negative, and in the opposite direction to AK if the given ratio is positive. Then KL meets AB in a point P such that the ratio $AP : PB$ is equal to the given ratio.

This result is an immediate deduction from the fact that the triangles APK, BPL are similar.

58. Anharmonic or Cross-Ratio.

A set of points upon a straight line is called a *Range*. A set of lines passing through a point is called a *Pencil*, and each line of the set is called a *Ray*.

If any four points $ABCD$ of a range be taken, the ratio of the ratios $\dfrac{AB}{BC}$ and $\dfrac{AD}{DC}$ is called the *Anharmonic* or *Cross-Ratio* of the points.

If any four rays OA, OB, OC, OD of a pencil be taken, the ratio of the ratios $\dfrac{\sin AOB}{\sin BOC}$ and $\dfrac{\sin AOD}{\sin DOC}$ is called the *Anharmonic* or *Cross-Ratio* of the pencil.

The *Cross-Ratio* of a range is expressed by the notation $\{ABCD\}$ which therefore denotes $\dfrac{AB}{BC} : \dfrac{AD}{DC}$ or $\dfrac{AB.DC}{BC.AD}$.

The Cross-Ratio of a pencil in like manner is expressed by $O\{ABCD\}$ which is equal to $\dfrac{\sin AOB}{\sin BOC} : \dfrac{\sin AOD}{\sin DOC}$.

It should be noted that the angles AOB, BOC have the same or opposite signs according as they are described by a line rotating from OA to OB, and from OB to OC in the same or opposite directions.

The Cross-Ratio of any four points of a range is equal to the Cross-Ratio of a pencil with any vertex O whose rays pass through the points.

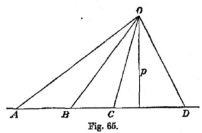

Fig. 65.

Let $ABCD$ be the points of the range. From any vertex O draw rays OA, OB, OC, OD, and let p be the length of the perpendicular from O upon the line $ABCD$.

Paying regard to sign, we have by expressing in two ways the areas of the triangle AOB, BOC, etc.

$$p.AB = OA.OB \sin AOB$$
$$p.BC = OB.OC \sin BOC$$
$$p.AD = OA.OD \sin AOD$$
$$p.DC = OD.OC \sin DOC.$$

7—2

Hence $\qquad \dfrac{AB}{BC} : \dfrac{AD}{DC} = \dfrac{\sin AOB}{\sin BOC} : \dfrac{\sin AOD}{\sin DOC},$

or $\qquad\qquad \{ABCD\} = O\,\{ABCD\}.$

Conversely if any pencil of rays be cut by a transversal, the cross-ratio of the pencil is equal to the cross-ratio of the range formed by the points of intersection.

59. *The Cross-Ratio of a Range of Points or of a Pencil of Rays is unaltered by projection.*

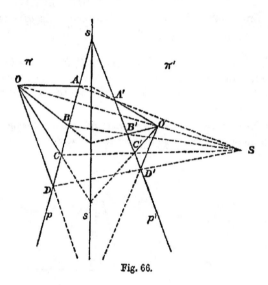

Fig. 66.

Let the pencil OA, OB, OC, OD lie in a plane π and cut any transversal p in the points $ABCD$. With any vertex of projection S project on to the plane π'; let O', A', B', C', D' correspond to O, A, B, C, D, and p' to p.

Then since p' and p are both transversals of the projecting pencil of rays SA, SB, SC, SD, we have

$$\{ABCD\} = S\,\{ABCD\} = S\,\{A'B'C'D'\} = \{A'B'C'D'\}.$$

Also

$$O\,\{ABCD\} = \{ABCD\} = \{A'B'C'D'\} = O'\,\{A'B'C'D'\}.$$

If I be the point at infinity on the line p, and if it project into I' upon the line p', we have

$$\frac{A'B'}{B'C'} : \frac{A'I'}{I'C'} = \frac{AB}{BC} : \frac{AI}{IC}.$$

But $AI \cdot IC = -1$; hence $\{A'B'C'I'\} = -\frac{AB}{BC}$, or any cross-ratio may be expressed as the ratio of two segments of a line.

60. *Given three points A, B, C on a line p, to find a fourth point D on the line, so that $\{ABCD\}$ may have a given value.*

Let the given value be equal in magnitude to the ratio $X : Y$ when X and Y are given lines. From A draw a line in any direction, on it take AB' equal to X, and $B'C'$ equal to Y, AB' and $B'C'$ being measured in the same or opposite directions according as the given ratio is negative or positive. Let BB', CC' meet in S and through S draw a line parallel to AC'; it will meet p in the required point D.

For by the construction D corresponds to the point at infinity upon the line AC', and S being the vertex of projection

$$\{ABCD\} = \{AB'C'\infty\} = -\frac{AB'}{B'C'} = -\frac{X}{Y}.$$

Hence $\{ABCD\}$ has the assigned value.

61. Harmonic Section. When the cross-ratio of four points A, B, C, D is equal to -1, the range is said to be *Harmonic*. In this case, by definition $\frac{AB}{BC} = -\frac{AD}{DC}$, and therefore the segment AC is divided internally and externally in the same ratio by the points B and D. AC is said to be a Harmonic Mean between AB and AD.

Since the above relation may be written in the form

$$\frac{DC}{CB} = -\frac{DA}{AB},$$

it follows that C and A divide the segment DB harmonically, and that DB is a Harmonic Mean between DC and DA.

A and C are said to be *harmonically conjugate* with respect to B and D, and conversely B and D are harmonically conjugate with respect to A and C.

The harmonic conjugate of the point at infinity with respect to A and C is the bisector of the segment AC.

A Harmonic Pencil is one which divides any transversal harmonically. It follows from Art. 59 that if a pencil divides one transversal harmonically it divides all transversals in the same manner.

If $O(ABCD)$ is a harmonic pencil, the rays OB, OD are harmonically conjugate with respect to OA, OC.

62   *If the angle between a pair of conjugate rays OA, OC be bisected by OB, then OB is at right angles to its conjugate OD.* For if a transversal be drawn parallel to OD meeting the other rays in A, B, C; B being conjugate to the point at infinity on the transversal will bisect AC. Hence since OB bisects both the angle AOC and the line AC it must be at right angles to AC, that is to OD.

Conversely if a pair of conjugate rays be at right angles, they bisect the angles between the other pair.

If $(ABCD)$ be a harmonic range, and O the middle point of AC, then $OB . OD = OC^2$.

Since $\dfrac{AB}{BC} = -\dfrac{AD}{DC},\quad \dfrac{AO+OB}{OC-OB} = \dfrac{AO+OD}{OD-OC},$

or $\dfrac{OC+OB}{OC-OB} = \dfrac{OC+OD}{OD-OC}.$

Hence $\dfrac{OC}{OB} = \dfrac{OD}{OC}$ or $OB . OD = OC^2.$

Conversely if O is the middle point of AC and $OB . OD = OC^2$, it follows that $(ABCD)$ is harmonic.

If $(ABCD)$ be a harmonic range, then

$$\frac{2}{AC} = \frac{1}{AB} + \frac{1}{AD}.$$

Since $\{ABCD\}$ is equal to -1,

$$\frac{AB}{BC} = -\frac{AD}{DC},$$

or $$\frac{AB}{AC-AB} = +\frac{AD}{AD-AC}.$$

Hence $2AB \cdot AD = AC \cdot AB + AC \cdot AD,$

and therefore $\dfrac{2}{AC} = \dfrac{1}{AB} + \dfrac{1}{AD}.$

In the same manner it may be shown that

$$\frac{2}{CA} = \frac{1}{CB} + \frac{1}{CD},$$

$$\frac{2}{BD} = \frac{1}{BA} + \frac{1}{BC},$$

and $\dfrac{2}{DB} = \dfrac{1}{DA} + \dfrac{1}{DC}.$

63. Harmonic Property of a Complete Quadrangle.

A *complete quadrangle* is a figure formed by four points called the *vertices* which are joined by six lines called the *sides* of the quadrangle. The sides joining opposite pairs of vertices meet in three points called the *diagonal points* of the quadrangle.

The lines joining any diagonal point to the other two are harmonically conjugate with respect to the sides meeting in that diagonal point.

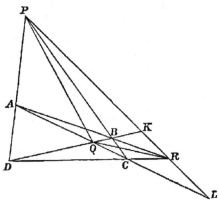

Fig. 67.

Let $ABCD$ be the quadrangle, P, Q, R the diagonal points; then $P(AQBR)$ is a harmonic pencil.

Let DB meet PR at K, and project PR to infinity. The quadrangle is then projected into a parallelogram $A'B'C'D'$, and

Q' will bisect $D'B'$; hence Q' is harmonically conjugate to the point at infinity upon $D'B'$, that is to K' the projection of K. Hence $(D'Q'B'K')$ and therefore $(DQBK)$ is harmonic. Therefore also the pencil $P(DQBK) = P(AQBR)$ is harmonic.

64.   Harmonic Property of a complete Quadrilateral.

A *complete quadrilateral* is a figure formed by four lines called the *sides* which meet in six points called the *vertices* of the quadrilateral. The vertices formed by the intersections of opposite pairs of sides are joined by three lines called the *diagonals* of the quadrilateral.

Any diagonal is divided by the other two in points harmonically conjugate with respect to the vertices upon that diagonal.

In the figure of the preceding theorem we may take AB, BC, CD, DA to be the sides of the quadrilateral, then A, B, C, D, P, R are the vertices, and AC, BD, PR the diagonals. It has then been shown that the diagonal DB is divided harmonically at Q and R, that is by the other two diagonals.

65. *If $(ABCD)$, $(AB'C'D')$ be two harmonic ranges upon different lines, the point A being common to both, then BB', CC', DD' will be concurrent and likewise BD', CC', $B'D$.*

Let BB', CC' meet at S; join SD and if it does not meet the line of the second range in D', let it meet it in D_1'. Then since $(ABCD)$ is harmonic, so also is the pencil $S(ABCD)$ and therefore $(AB'C'D_1')$ is harmonic. Hence $\{AB'C'D_1'\} = \{AB'C'D'\}$ and therefore D_1' coincides with D'.

Again let BD', $B'D$ intersect at S', and let CS' meet the line of the second range in C_1'.

Then $\{ABCD\} = S'\{ABCD\} = \{AD'C_1'B'\} = -1$.
But $\{AB'C'D'\} = -1$ and therefore

$$\frac{AD'}{D'C_1'} \cdot \frac{B'C_1'}{AB'} = -1 \text{ and } \frac{AB'}{B'C'} \cdot \frac{D'C'}{AD'} = -1.$$

Comparing the two equations we see that C' must coincide with C_1'. Therefore CC' also passes through S'.

66. *To construct the harmonic conjugate of a point with respect to two given points in the same line with it, and the harmonic conjugate of a ray with respect to two rays concurrent with it.*

Let A be the given point, B and D the points with respect to which the conjugate of A is required.

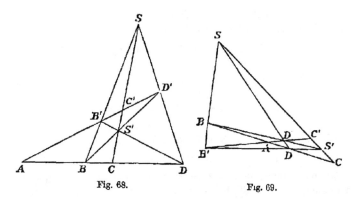

Fig. 68.   Fig. 69.

Through B and D draw any two lines meeting at S, and through A draw any line cutting SB, SD at B' and D' respectively. Join BD', $B'D$ and let them intersect at S', then SS' will intersect BD at C the point conjugate to A.

If three concurrent rays SA, SB, SD are given, and the ray conjugate to SA with respect to SB and SD is required, we find it by drawing two transversals ABD, $AB'D'$. If BD', $B'D$ intersect in S', then SS' is the conjugate to SA.

1. *Given a segment AC bisected at B, draw through a given point S a line parallel to AC.*

Join SA, SB, SC and construct the ray harmonically conjugate to SB with respect to SA and SC.

2. *Given a segment AC and a line parallel to it bisect AC.*

3. *Given two lines AB and CD which meet at an inaccessible point S construct a line passing through S and a given point P.*

Through P draw any two lines KPL', LPK' meeting AB and CD in KL, $K'L'$ respectively. Let LL', KK' intersect in S'. Then $S(APCS')$ is a harmonic pencil.

Through S' draw any third line $S'MM'$ intersecting AB and CD in M and M'. Let ML', LM' meet at Q; then $S(AQCS')$ is harmonic, and therefore SPQ is a straight line.

4. *Given two parallel lines draw through a given point P a line parallel to them.*

5. *Given two points A and B and a given line p determine the point of intersection of p with AB without drawing AB.*

From A and B draw k and l' respectively intersecting upon p, also l and k'. Let s' be the line joining the intersections of kk' and ll'. Upon s' take any point and from it draw m to A and m' to B. Let q be the line joining the intersections of lm' and $l'm$. Then the intersection of pq is upon AB.

67. Homographic Ranges and Pencils.

Two ranges of points $ABC...$, and $A'B'C'...$ on the same or different lines, such that to every point P of the one, corresponds one point P' of the other are said to be *homographic* when the cross-ratio of any four points of the one is equal to the cross-ratio of the four corresponding points of the other.

A similar definition holds for homographic pencils.

It is convenient to use the notation $\{ABC...\} = \{A'B'C'...\}$ to denote that the ranges $(ABC...)$, $(A'B'C'...)$ are homographic, and the notation $O\{ABC...\} = O'\{A'B'C'...\}$ to denote that the pencils $O(ABC...)$, $O'(A'B'C'...)$ are homographic.

68. *If the lines joining three pairs of corresponding points on two homographic ranges are concurrent in a point S, all the lines joining pairs of corresponding points are concurrent in the same point.*

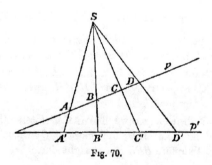

Fig. 70.

Let $(ABCD...)$ $(A'B'C'D'...)$ be two homographic ranges upon the lines p and p', and let AA', BB', CC' meet at S. Let SD meet p' at D_1'.

Then $\{ABCD\} = S\{ABCD\} = \{A'B'C'D_1'\}$.

But $\{ABCD\} = \{A'B'C'D'\}$ since the ranges are homographic, and therefore D_1' and D' coincide. Hence DD' passes through S, and the same is true of the line joining any other pair of corresponding points.

In the same manner may be proved the following theorem:

69   *If the points of intersection of three pairs of corresponding rays of two homographic pencils are collinear on a line s, all the points of intersection of corresponding pairs of rays lie upon the same line.*

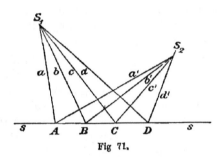

Fig 71.

When Homographic Ranges or Pencils are so placed that the lines joining corresponding points are concurrent or the points of intersection of corresponding rays are collinear, the Ranges or Pencils are said to be in *perspective*, or to be in *projective* position. It is clear that the point of concurrence in the one case and the line of collinearity in the other are respectively a centre of projection and an axis of projection.

70.   *If two homographic ranges $(ABC...)$, $(A'B'C'...)$ on different lines have one pair of corresponding points coincident, then the ranges are in perspective.*

Let A coincide with A' and let BB', CC' intersect in S, then as in the previous case we can show that DD' also passes through S.

In like manner it may be proved that:

If two homographic pencils $O(ABC...)$, $O'(A'B'C'...)$ have one pair of corresponding rays coincident, then the pencils are in perspective.

Let OA, $O'A'$ be coincident corresponding rays. Let OB, $O'B'$ intersect in M, OC, $O'C'$ in N and let MN meet OA in L. Let OD, $O'D'$ be another pair of rays meeting MN in K and K' respectively. Then

$$O\{ABCD\} = \{LMNK\}$$

and $$O'\{A'B'C'D'\} = \{LMNK'\};$$

therefore K coincides with K'.

71   When Homographic Pencils are not in perspective, not more than two intersections of corresponding rays will lie in a given straight line; and when Homographic Ranges are not in perspective, not more than two lines joining pairs of corresponding points will pass through a given point.

Hence the locus of the points of intersection of corresponding rays of homographic pencils not in perspective is a curve which any straight line intersects in two points only; and the envelope of the lines joining pairs of corresponding points on two homographic ranges not in perspective is a curve such that only two tangents can be drawn to it from a given point. These properties are characteristic of the circle and of the curves derived from it by projection, the conic sections.

A curve such that a straight line intersects it in two points only is of the second degree; and a curve such that only two tangents can be drawn to it from a given point is of the second order.

72   *If $(ABC...)$, $(A'B'C'...)$ be two homographic ranges upon different lines p and p', and if any two pairs of corresponding points such as AA', BB' be joined cross-wise, A to B' and A' to B by lines meeting at L, then all points such as L lie upon a fixed line called the Homographic Axis.*

Let AB', $A'B$ intersect at L; AC', $A'C$ at M; and AD', $A'D$ at N. Then since $\{ABCD\} = \{A'B'C'D'\}$,

it follows that $A'\{ABCD\} = A\{A'B'C'D'\}$.

Hence since the ray AA' is common to the two pencils, L, M, N must be collinear.

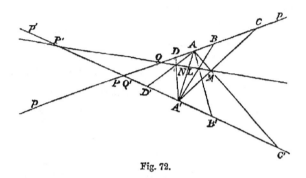

Fig. 72.

Let the lines p and p' intersect at a point named P or Q' according as it is regarded as belonging to the first or second range, and let P', Q be the points corresponding to P and Q'. Then since AP', $A'P$ intersect at P', and AQ', $A'Q$ at Q, it follows from the above that P', Q must be collinear with $L, M,$ and N. But P' and Q are determined without special reference to A and A', and hence all other points of cross-wise intersection, such as of BC' and $B'C$ must also lie on this line.

From the above theorem we obtain a method of constructing pairs of corresponding points in homographic ranges. For let AA', BB', CC' be three pairs of corresponding points of two ranges. Let AB', $A'B$ intersect at L, and AC', $A'C$ at M. Then to find the point D' corresponding to any fourth point D, we draw $A'D$ intersecting LM at N; AN then passes through the required point D'.

If AA', BB', CC', ... be pairs of corresponding points of two homographic ranges upon the same line p, we can take any vertex of projection S and project the range $(ABC...)$ into a range $(A_1B_1C_1...)$ upon a line p_1. Then

$$\{A'B'C'...\} = \{ABC...\} = \{A_1B_1C_1...\}.$$

Hence $(A'B'C'...)$, $(A_1B_1C_1...)$ are homographic, and the point D' corresponding to any point D_1, the projection of D may be found as before.

If two homographic pencils $O(ABC...)$, $O'(A'B'C'...)$ have three pairs of corresponding rays given, then to find the ray $O'D'$ corresponding to any ray OD, we cut the pencils by two transversals in the ranges of corresponding points $(ABC...)$ $(A'B'C'...)$.

If OD meets the first transversal in D, we find as above the point D' corresponding to D, and then $O'D'$ is the required ray.

73. Anharmonic Properties of Points on a Circle or Conic.

The Cross-Ratio of the pencil formed by joining any point on a conic to four fixed points on the conic is constant, and is equal to the cross-ratio of the range in which the tangents at these points are cut by any other tangent.

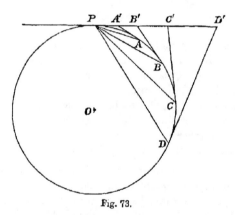

Fig. 73.

We shall prove this theorem for the case of a circle, then since cross-ratios are unaltered by projection, it will be true also for a conic.

Let $ABCD$ be the fixed points, and P any other point on the circle. Then since the angles APB, BPC, CPD are constant for all positions of P, the value of $P\{ABCD\}$ must be constant.

Next let the tangents at $ABCD$ cut the tangent at P in the points $A'B'C'D'$. If O be the centre of the circle, the angles $A'OB'$, $B'OC'$, $C'OD'$, are equal to APB, BPC, CPD respectively and are therefore constant. Hence

$$\{A'B'C'D'\} = O\{A'B'C'D'\} = P\{ABCD\}.$$

If $ABCDS_1S_2$ are six points on a conic, we see that the pencils $S_1(ABCD)$, $S_2(ABCD)$ are homographic, A, B, C, D being the intersections of corresponding rays. But it has been shown in Art 71 that the locus of the intersections of corresponding rays of homographic pencils is a curve of the second degree, hence a conic is of the second degree.

Also if a, b, c, d, s_1, s_2 are six tangents to a conic, the ranges determined by a, b, c, d on s_1 and s_2 are homographic, a, b, c, d being the lines joining corresponding points. Hence by Art. 71 it appears that a conic is a curve of the second order.

74. *To project the locus of the intersection of two homographic pencils into a circle, the pencils being neither concentric nor in perspective.*

Let the pencils be $S_1(PQR...)$ and $S_2(PQR...)$. Since the pencils are not in perspective the ray S_2S_1 whose vertex is S_2 will correspond to a ray S_1T, and this ray will be the tangent at S_1 to the locus of the intersections of the pencils.

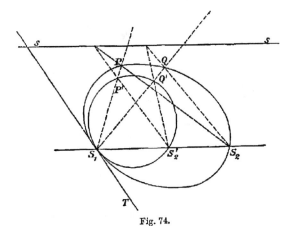

Fig. 74.

Describe a circle touching S_1T at S_1 and cutting the rays $S_1(S_2, P, Q...)$ in S_2', P', Q' respectively.

Then $S_2(S_1PQ...) = S_1(TPQ...) = S_1(TP'Q'...) = S_1(S_1P'Q'...)$
$$= S_2'(S_1P'Q'...).$$

Hence $S_2(S_1 PQ...)$ and $S_2'(S_1 P'Q'...)$ are homographic pencils and they have the ray $S_2 S_2' S_1$ common; therefore the intersections of the corresponding rays will lie in a straight line s.

We see then that the lines PP', QQ', $...S_2 S_2'$, joining pairs of corresponding points all pass through the same point S_1, while the points of intersection of pairs of corresponding lines such as $S_2 P$, $S_2' P'$; $S_2 Q$, $S_2' Q'$, lie on a straight line.

Hence S_1 is the centre of projection, and s the axis of projection of the curve $(S_1 S_2 PQ...)$ and the circle $(S_1 S_2' P'Q'...)$.

Hence the locus of the intersection of two homographic pencils is the projection of a circle, that is a conic section.

75. *To project into a circle the envelope of the lines joining corresponding points of two homographic ranges upon different lines and not in perspective.*

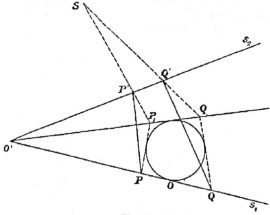

Fig. 75.

Let the ranges be $(PQR...)$ and $(P'Q'R'...)$ upon the lines s_1 and s_2. Let O' be the point of intersection of s_1 and s_2 regarded as a point of the range upon s_2, and let O be the corresponding point upon s_1. Describe any circle touching s_1 at O, and draw tangents to it from O', P, Q, R,.... Let P_1, Q_1, R_1,... be the points of intersection of the tangents from P, Q, R with that from O'.

Then $\{O'P'Q'R'...\} = \{OPQR...\} = \{O'P_1 Q_1 R_1 ...\}$.

Therefore the ranges $(O'P'Q'R'...)$ and $(O'P_1Q_1R_1...)$ are homographic, and since they have a common point O', the lines joining corresponding points will meet in a point S.

But the points of intersection of corresponding lines $P'P$, P_1P; $Q'Q$, Q_1Q, ... all lie on the line s_1, hence the figures formed by these lines are in perspective, S being the centre of projection and s_1 the axis of projection. Hence since the lines P_1P, Q_1Q, ... touch a circle, the lines $P'P$, $Q'Q$, ... touch a conic.

76. Homographic Ranges on a Conic. If there be two sets of points $(ABC...)$, $(A'B'C'...)$ on a conic such that to each point of one set corresponds one point of the other, then if the cross-ratio of the pencil formed by joining any four points of the one set to any point on the conic is equal to the cross-ratio of the pencil formed by joining the four corresponding points of the second set to any point on the conic, the two sets of points are said to be *Homographic*.

77. *If* $(ABC...)$, $(A'B'C'...)$ *be two homographic ranges on a conic, the points of intersection of the lines joining crosswise two pairs of corresponding points (such as AB', $A'B$), all lie on a straight line called the homographic axis.*

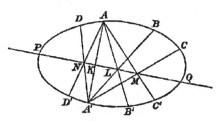

Fig. 76.

Let AB', $A'B$ intersect in L, AC', $A'C$ in M, AD', $A'D$ in N. Then the pencils $A\ (A'B'C'D')$, $A'\ (ABCD)$ are of equal cross-ratio and have the ray AA' common, hence L, M, N lie in a straight line. Let this line cut the conic in the points P and Q and AA' in K. Then $A\ (A'B'C'P) = \{KLMP\} = A'\ \{ABCP\}$. Therefore the point P regarded as belonging to one range corresponds to itself regarded as belonging to the second range. In like manner Q corresponds to itself. P and Q are therefore the common points of the two ranges.

M. D.   8

We see then that the intersections of all the crosswise joins of corresponding points must lie upon PQ, which is the homographic axis of the two ranges.

Given three pairs of corresponding points ABC, $A'B'C'$ of two homographic ranges, to construct the point D' corresponding to D.

As before let AB', $A'B$ intersect in L, AC', $A'C$ in M. Let $A'D$ meet LM in N, then AN will meet the conic in the required point D'.

78. *To construct the common points of two homographic ranges upon a straight line.*

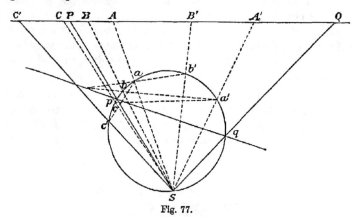

Fig. 77.

Let the ranges be $(ABC\ldots)$, $(A'B'C'\ldots)$. Draw any circle, take any point S on it, and draw SA, SB, SC, ...; SA', SB', SC', ... cutting the circle in a, b, c,..., a', b', c',...; $(a, b, c,...)$, $(a', b', c',...)$ are two homographic ranges. Let their homographic axis meet the circle in p, q. Then P, Q, the points where Sp, Sq meet the line are the common points of the homographic ranges.

The common rays of two homographic pencils may be found by determining the common points of the ranges they make on any transversal.

III. CONSTRUCTION OF A CONIC SATISFYING GIVEN CONDITIONS.

79. In general a conic can be constructed satisfying *five* conditions, such as passing through five given points or touching five given lines.

Special cases arise when some of the points or lines are coincident or when they are at infinity.

A tangent and its point of contact are equivalent to two coincident points or to two coincident tangents.

The direction of an asymptote is equivalent to a point at infinity. The position of an asymptote is equivalent to two coincident points at infinity.

If the curve is a parabola, then one tangent, the line at infinity, is given.

If the direction of the axis of a parabola is given, this is equivalent to having given a tangent and its point of contact.

Whenever by considerations such as the foregoing it can be seen that the data are equivalent to five points or to five tangents, the conic can be constructed by a modification of the method used in the general case.

80. *Construction of a conic of which five points $S_1 S_2 ABC$ are given.*

It has been shown that a conic is the locus of the points of intersection of corresponding rays of two homographic pencils not in perspective. Now the correspondence between two homographic pencils is completely determined when three pairs of

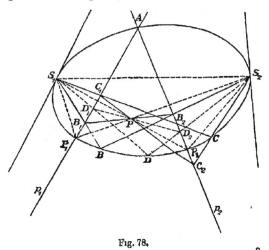

Fig. 78.

8—2

corresponding rays are given. This is equivalent to having given the vertices of the pencils and the three points of intersection of corresponding rays, five points in all, and therefore a conic is determined by five points.

We shall take S_1S_2 to be the vertices and ABC to be the points of intersection of pencils.

Through A draw any two lines p_1 and p_2. Let S_1B, S_1C meet p_1 in B_1 and C_1, and let S_2B, S_2C meet p_2 in B_2 and C_2. Join B_1B_2, C_1C_2 and let them intersect at P. Through P draw any line meeting p_1 in D_1 and p_2 in D_2, then S_1D_1 and S_2D_2 will meet at a point D on the conic.

By the construction $S_1\{ABCD\} = S_1\{AB_1C_1D_1\} = \{AB_1C_1D_1\}$
$= P\{AB_1C_1D_1\} = P\{AB_2C_2D_2\} = S_2\{AB_2C_2D_2\} = S_2\{ABCD\}$.

Hence $S_1(ABCD)$ and $S_2(ABCD)$ are homographic pencils, and the locus of D will be a conic through S_1S_2ABC.

If S_1P meet p_2 in P_2, then P_2 is a point on the locus. Since p_2 is quite arbitrary, we have found in this way the point in which any line drawn through one of the given points meets the conic.

The ray through S_1 corresponding to S_2S_1 through S_2 is the tangent at S_1, for it is the limiting position of S_1D when D is indefinitely close to S_1.

81. *Construction of a conic of which five tangents s_1s_2abc are given*

It has been shown that a conic is the envelope of the lines joining corresponding points of two homographic ranges not in perspective. Now the correspondence between two homographic ranges is completely determined when three pairs of corresponding points are given. This is equivalent to having given the lines of the ranges and the three lines joining corresponding points, five lines in all, and therefore a conic is determined by five tangents.

We shall take s_1s_2 to be the lines of the ranges and abc to be the lines joining corresponding points.

Upon a take any two points P_1 and P_2. Let b_1 and c_1 be the lines joining P_1 to the intersections of s_1, b, and s_1, c respectively; and let b_2 and c_2 be the lines joining P_2 to the intersections of s_2, b, and s_2, c respectively. Let p be the line joining the points of intersection of b_1, b_2 and c_1, c_2. Upon p take any point, let d_1

be the line joining it to P_1 and d_2 the line joining it to p_2, then the line d joining the intersections of s_1, d_1, and s_2, d_2 will be a tangent to the conic.

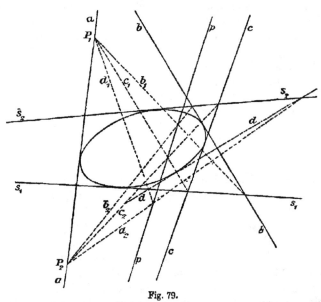

Fig. 79.

Denote by $s \{a, b, c, d\}$ the cross-ratio of the range made by any lines a, b, c, d with a line s, and by $\{abcd\}$ the cross-ratio of a pencil whose rays are $abcd$.

With this notation we see that in the above construction we have

$$s_1\{abcd\} = s_1\{ab_1c_1d_1\} = \{ab_1c_1d_1\} = p\{ab_1c_1d_1\} = p\{ab_2c_2d_2\}$$
$$= s_2\{ab_2c_2d_2\} = s_2\{abcd\}.$$

Hence $s_1(abcd)$ and $s_2(abcd)$ are homographic ranges, and the envelope of d will be a conic touching s_1s_2abc.

If p_2 is the line joining P_2 to the intersection of s_1, p, then p_1 is a tangent to the curve. Since P_2 is quite arbitrary we have found in this way the tangent drawn to the curve from a point on one of the given tangents.

The point of s_1 corresponding to the intersection of s_1s_2 regarded as a point of s_2 is the point of contact of s_1 with the conic, for it is the limiting position of the intersection of s_1d, when d is indefinitely close to s_1.

82. Pascal's Theorem. *If a hexagon be inscribed in a conic the points of intersections of opposite sides are collinear.*

When five points are given a sixth point taken arbitrarily will not in general lie on the conic through the five points. The condition that six points may lie on a conic may be obtained from the construction in Art. 80. Let $S_1 S_2 A P_1 P_2 D$ be the six points, $P_1 P_2$ being the points where the lines p_1, p_2 meet the conic. The condition that D may be on the curve is that $D_1 P D_2$ be collinear. This condition may be expressed in the following form. If we take the points in the order $S_1 P_2 A P_1 S_2 D S_1$, a hexagon is formed and $D_1 P D_2$ are the points of intersections of opposite sides. Hence we have Pascal's theorem:—If a hexagon be inscribed in a conic the points of intersections of opposite sides are collinear.

83. Brianchon's Theorem. *If a hexagon circumscribe a conic the lines joining the opposite points of intersections of tangents are concurrent.*

Let $s_1 s_2 a p_1 p_2 d$ be the six tangents, p_1 and p_2 being the tangents drawn from P_1 and P_2 to the conic. The condition that d may be a tangent is that $d_1 p d_2$ be concurrent. This condition may be expressed in the following form. If we take the tangents in the order $s_1 p_2 a p_1 s_2 d$, a hexagon is formed and $d_1 p d_2$ are the lines joining opposite points of intersection of the tangents. Hence we have Brianchon's theorem.

84. Applications of Pascal's and Brianchon's Theorems.

Starting from one point of a hexagon the remaining points may be taken in $\frac{1}{2} \lfloor 5$ that is 60 ways, counting any order and its reverse as the same. Hence 60 hexagons can be formed with 6 points, and to each hexagon a line of collinearity, named a Pascal line, will correspond.

In like manner 60 hexagons can be formed from 6 lines, and to each one will correspond a point of concurrence. By supposing some of the points in a Pascal hexagon or the lines in a Brianchon hexagon to become coincident we obtain important results connected with tangents to conics.

It will be convenient in proving these theorems to denote by $AB'CA'BC'$ the points of the fundamental Pascal hexagon, and by $ab'ca'bc'$ the sides of the fundamental Brianchon hexagon.

85. *Given five points of a conic AB'CA'B to find where a line through A meets the conic.*

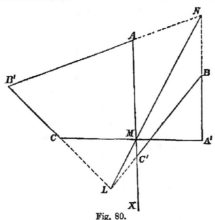

Fig. 80.

Let C' be the point required, the line AX being given. Let AB', $A'B$ intersect in N and AX, $A'C$ intersect in M. Join MN and let $B'C$ meet it in L. Then BL will meet AX' at the required point C'.

In this way any number of points on the conic could be found; but when a large number is required the construction of Art. 80 (due to Maclaurin) is preferable.

Given five tangents to a conic, ab'ca'b, to construct the tangent from a point on a to the conic.

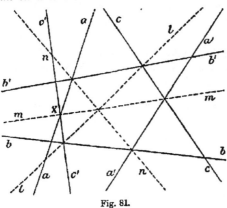

Fig. 81.

Let c' be the required tangent, the point X being given. Let n be the line joining the intersections of ab', $a'b$; and m the line joining the intersection of $a'c$ to X. Draw l through the intersections of nm and $b'c$. Then c' will be the line joining X to the intersection of bl.

86. *Given five points of a conic, to draw the tangent at any one of them.*

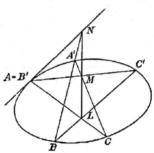

Fig. 82.

If we suppose two of the points AB' of the hexagon $AB'CA'BC'$ to become coincident, the limiting direction of AB' will be the tangent at A. This tangent will intersect $A'B$, the side opposite A, upon the Pascal line determined by the intersections of $B'C$, BC' and $C'A$, CA'.

Given five tangents to a conic to determine the point of contact of any one of them.

· If we suppose two of the sides ab' of the Brianchon hexagon $ab'ca'bc'$ to become coincident, the limiting position of the intersection of ab' will be the point of contact of the tangent. The line joining this point to the intersection of $a'b$, must pass through the intersections of the lines joining the intersection of $b'c$, bc' and of $c'a$, ca'.

87. *If a quadrilateral be inscribed in a conic, the tangents at opposite vertices intersect on a diagonal.*

If we suppose two pairs of points of a Pascal hexagon to become coincident the figure will become an inscribed quadrilateral with tangents at two vertices. Let AB' and $A'B$ be the two pairs of coincident points, the lines AB' and $A'B$ being in the limit the tangents at A and A'. These form a pair of opposite sides of the hexagon and their intersection must lie upon the line through the intersections of BC', $B'C$ and CA', $C'A$. This line in the limit is one of the diagonals of the quadrilateral $ACA'C'$.

If a quadrilateral circumscribe a conic, the line joining the points of contact of opposite sides passes through the intersection of the diagonals.

This may be proved by considering the limiting form of a Brianchon hexagon of which two pairs of sides have become coincident.

88. *Given four points on a conic and the tangent at one of them to construct the conic.*

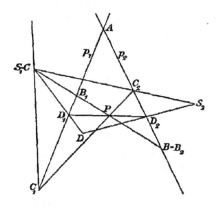

Fig. 83.

Let the points be ABS_1S_2 and let the tangent at S_1 be given. We may then regard S_1 as a double point, a fifth point C coinciding with it, so that the limiting position of S_1C is the tangent at S_1.

Proceed as in the general case drawing p_1, p_2 through A. The tangent at S_1 meets p_1 in C_1, and S_2S_1 meets p_2 in C_2. B_1 and B_2 are the points of intersection of S_1B and S_2B with p_1 and p_2 respectively. Let C_1C_2, B_1B_2 intersect at P, then any number of points may be found by drawing lines through P, cutting p_1 and p_2, such as D_1PD_2, and joining S_1D_1 and S_2D_2. D the intersection of S_1D_1 and S_2D_2 is a point on the conic.

Note. For simplicity p_1 and p_2 may be drawn through C and B which then may be taken as C_1 and B_1 respectively.

89. *Given four points and the direction of an asymptote to construct the conic.*

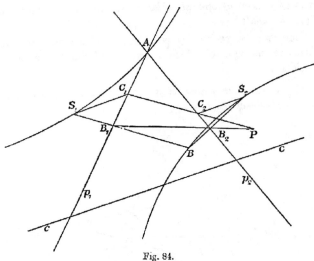

Fig. 84.

Let the points be ABS_1S_2 and let a line c be parallel to the asymptote. We may regard the point at infinity on this line as the fifth point C.

Proceed as in the general case; C_1 and C_2 will be the points where lines through S_1 and S_2 parallel to c meet p_1 and p_2.

Otherwise. Take S_1 to be the point at infinity on the given line s parallel to the asymptote, and let the other points be $ABCS_2$. Then BB_1 and CC_1 will be parallel to s. The asymptote is the ray through S_1 corresponding to the ray S_2S_1 through S_2. To construct it draw $S_2\sigma_2$ parallel to s meeting p_2 at σ_2, let σ_2P meet p_1 at σ_1, then the parallel to s through σ_1 is the asymptote.

90. *To construct a parabola, given three points and the direction of the axis.*

Let ABS_1 be the given points and let c be a line parallel to the axis. We may take C and S_2 to coincide at infinity upon c, then CS_2 will be the tangent at infinity.

Through A draw p_1 and p_2, and construct B_1 and B_2. $S_1 C_1$ is drawn parallel to c, and C_2 will be the point at infinity upon p_2.

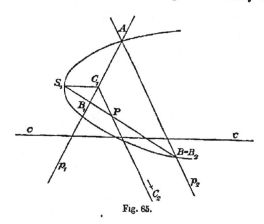

Fig. 85.

Hence P is the intersection of $B_1 B_2$ and the parallel to p_2 through C_1.

1. *Construct a conic touching two lines at given points and passing through another point.*

2. *Construct a conic, given two asymptotes and a point on the conic.*

3. *Construct a conic, given one asymptote, the direction of the other and two points.*

4. *Construct a conic, given three points, the tangent at one of them and the direction of an asymptote.*

5. *Given four points on a conic and the direction of an asymptote to find where a line parallel to an asymptote meets the conic.*

Take the four points to be $S_1 S_2 BC$, take A to be the point at infinity on the two lines parallel to the asymptote, and take the lines as p_1 and p_2.

6. *Given four points on a conic and the direction of one asymptote find the direction of the other.*

7. *Construct a parabola given two points, the tangent at one of them and the direction of the axis.*

91. It has been shown that when five points of a conic are given, the tangent at any one of them may be determined by an application of Pascal's theorem. (See Art. 86.)

In the following examples some of the points are coincident or at infinity.

1. *Given four points on a conic and the tangent at one of them, construct the tangent at any of the other points.*

2. *Given three points on a conic and the tangents at two of them, construct the tangent at the third point.*

3. *Given three points on a parabola and the direction of the axis, construct the tangent at any of the given points.*

4. *Given two points on a parabola, the tangent at one of them, and the direction of the axis, construct the tangent at the other point.*

5. *Given four points on a conic and the direction of an asymptote, construct the tangent at any of the points, and the asymptote.*

6. *Given three points on a conic and an asymptote, construct the tangent at any of the points.*

7. *Given three points on a conic and the directions of the two asymptotes, construct the asymptotes and the tangents at the points.*

8. *Given two points on a conic, one asymptote and the direction of the other, construct the second asymptote.*

9. *Given a point on a conic and both asymptotes, construct the tangent at the point.*

92 It has been shown that when five tangents to a conic are given, the points of contact may be determined by an application of Brianchon's theorem. (See Art. 83.)

In the following examples some of the tangents are coincident or at infinity.

1. *Given four tangents and the point of contact of one of them, determine the points of contact of the others.*

2. *Given three tangents and the points of contact of two of them, determine the point of contact of the third.*

3. *Given four tangents to a parabola, determine the points of contact and the direction of the axis.*

4. *Given three tangents to a parabola and the point of contact of one of them, determine the points of contact of the others.*

5. *Given two tangents to a parabola and their points of contact, determine the direction of the axis.*

6. *Given three tangents and an asymptote, determine the points of contact.*

7. *Given a tangent and two asymptotes, determine the point of contact of the tangent.*

IV. Involution.

93. *Definition.* Let O be a fixed point on a line, and A, A'; B, B'; C, C'; ... pairs of points on the line such that

$$OA . OA' = OB . OB' = OC . OC' = ... = \text{a constant,}$$

then these points are said to form a system in *involution*. O is called the *centre* of the involution, and corresponding points such as A, A' are said to be *conjugate* to one another.

The point at infinity is conjugate to the centre.

If $OA . OA' = + k^2$, A and A' will be on the same side of the centre, and there will be two points K_1 and K_2 one on each side of the centre such that $OK_1^2 = OK_2^2 = k^2$. These points are called the *double points* or *foci* of the involution. Since

$$OA . OA' = OK_1^2 = OK_2^2$$

we see from Art. 62 that A and A' are harmonically conjugate with respect to the two foci.

If $OA . OA' = - k^2$, A and A' will lie on opposite sides of the centre and no real foci exist.

If the foci are real, and one is at infinity, the centre is also at infinity. The finite focus will then bisect the distance between pairs of conjugate points.

Pencils in Involution. If any point S be joined to the points of a range in involution, the pencil of rays so formed is said to be in *involution*.

The rays drawn to the double points of the range are the double rays of the pencil.

94. *Given two pairs of conjugate points of a range in involution
to find the point conjugate to any given point.*

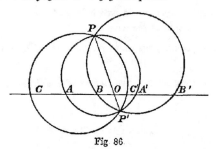

Fig 86

Let A, A'; B, B' be the given pairs of points; it is required
to find the point C' conjugate to any other given point C.

Through AA' draw any circle, and through BB' any other
circle intersecting the first one in P and P'. Let PP' cut the
line of the range in O. Then O is the centre of the involution,
for $OA . OA' = OP . OP' = OB . OB'$.

Hence a circle drawn through CPP' will cut the line of the
range in the required point C'.

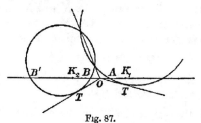

Fig. 87.

When double points exist, they may be found by drawing
a tangent OT from the centre to the circle through AA'. Then
the double points K_1, K_2 are the points of the range such that
$OK_1^2 = OK_2^2 = OT^2$.

95. *If any number of points be in involution the cross-ratio
of any four points is equal to that of their four conjugates.*

Let A, B, C, D be any four points and let their distances from
the centre be a, b, c, d respectively. Then the distances of their
conjugates A', B', C', D' are $\dfrac{k}{a}$, $\dfrac{k}{b}$, $\dfrac{k}{c}$, $\dfrac{k}{d}$ respectively.

But $\qquad \{ABCD\} = \dfrac{(b-a)(c-d)}{(c-b)(d-a)},$

and

$$\{A'B'C'D'\} = \frac{\left(\dfrac{k}{b} - \dfrac{k}{a}\right)\left(\dfrac{k}{c} - \dfrac{k}{d}\right)}{\left(\dfrac{k}{c} - \dfrac{k}{b}\right)\left(\dfrac{k}{d} - \dfrac{k}{a}\right)} = \frac{(b-a)(c-d)}{(c-b)(d-a)} = \{ABCD\}.$$

By means of this theorem we can find whether six points are in involution. For if P, P' are conjugate points of the involution determined by A, A'; B, B'

$$\{AA'BP\} = \{A'AB'P'\}.$$

Since the cross-ratios of ranges and pencils are unaltered by projection, it follows that ranges and pencils in involution are projected into ranges and pencils in involution.

96. *If a system of chords of a circle be concurrent, the lines joining the extremities of the chords to any point on the circle form a pencil in involution.*

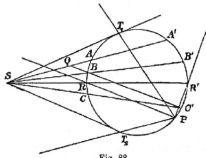

Fig. 88.

Let AA', BB', CC',... be chords of a circle which meet at a point S, and let P be any point of the circle.

Let BC' meet AA' in Q.

Then $\qquad P\{AA'BC\} = C'\{AA'BC\} = \{AA'QS\};$

and $\qquad P\{A'AB'C'\} = B\{A'AB'C'\} = \{A'ASQ\}.$

But $\qquad \{AA'QS\} = \dfrac{AA'}{A'Q} \times \dfrac{SQ}{AS} = \{A'ASQ\}.$

Hence $P\{AA'BC\} = P\{A'AB'C'\}$ and therefore the pencil $P(AA', BB', CC')$ is in involution.

If the point S be outside the circle, then the rays PT_1, PT_2 drawn to the points of contact of the tangents ST_1, ST_2 will be the double rays of the pencil.

Whatever be the position of S one chord RSR' will pass through the centre of the circle and the rays PR, PR' are at right angles. Hence *there always exists one pair of conjugate rays of a pencil in involution at right angles to one another.*

If S is the centre of the circle all conjugate rays are at right angles. But S will be the centre if two pairs of conjugate rays are at right angles, and therefore if two pairs of conjugate rays are at right angles, all pairs of conjugate rays are at right angles.

97.   *The opposite sides of a quadrangle cut any straight line in a range in involution.*

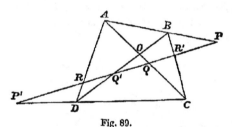

Fig. 89.

Let $ABCD$ be the quadrangle, and let any straight line cut AB, CD, AC, BD, AD, BC in P, P', Q, Q', R, R', respectively. Then (PP', QQ', RR') is a range in involution.

Let AC and BD intersect at O.   Then
$$A\{PRQQ'\} = A\{BDOQ'\} = C\{BDOQ'\} = C\{R'P'QQ'\}$$
$$= C\{P'R'Q'Q\}.$$

Hence $\{PRQQ'\} = \{P'R'Q'Q\}$ and therefore the range is in involution.

By means of this theorem the point conjugate to a given point of a range in involution may be found by a construction involving straight lines only.

Let the involution be defined by the two pairs of points A, A'; B, B'; and let it be required to find the point P' conjugate to a given point P.

Through P draw any line, and upon it take any two points K and L. Join KA, KB', LA', LB. Let KA and LB intersect at

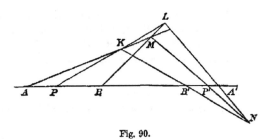

Fig. 90.

M and KB' and LA' at N. Then NM will cut AA' in the required point P'. For $KLMN$ is a quadrangle and therefore its sides are cut by the line AA' in a range of points in involution.

98 The straight lines joining any point to pairs of opposite vertices of a quadrilateral form a pencil in involution.

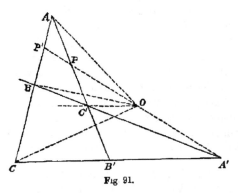

Fig 91.

Let A, A'; B, B'; C, C' be the pairs of opposite vertices of a quadrilateral, and let O be any point; then the pencil $O(AA', BB', CC')$ is in involution.

Let OA' meet AB', AC in P and P'. Then
$$O\{AA'B'C'\} = O\{APB'C'\} = A'\{APB'C'\} = A'\{AP'CB\}$$
$$= A'\{P'ABC\} = O\{P'ABC\} = O\{A'ABC\}.$$
Hence the pencil $O\{AA', BB', CC'\}$ is in involution.

V. POLE AND POLAR.

99   If a chord of a circle be drawn through a given point A, cutting the circle at B and B', and if A' be the harmonic conjugate of A with respect to B and B', then the locus of A' for different positions of the chord is called the *polar* of A with respect to the circle.

It will be proved that the *polar* of a point with respect to a circle is a straight line, and the point is called the *pole* of this line.

If the point A be outside the circle, two positions of the chord ABB' are the limiting positions of tangency. In this case B, B' and A' coincide. Hence the polar of a point outside a circle passes through the points of contact of the tangents drawn from the point.

If O be the middle point of the chord BB', then since A and A' are harmonic conjugates, $OB^2 = OA \cdot OA'$. If the chord be a diameter, A and A' lie upon a radius at distances from the centre O such that $OA \cdot OA' = (\text{radius})^2$ and they are then said to be *inverse* with respect to the circle. Of the two points one will be within the circle and the other without the circle. Let A be within, and draw AL at right angles to OA cutting the circle at T and T'. Then the triangles OAT, $OA'T$ are similar and the angle OTA' is equal to the angle OAT. Therefore $A'T$ and $A'T'$ are the tangents to the circle from A'. Hence TT' are points on the polar of A', and we proceed to prove that AL is the polar of A' and that a line $A'L'$ at right angles to OA' is the polar of A.

100. *If A and A' are inverse points with respect to a circle, then any chord of the circle drawn through one of them A' meets the straight line drawn through A at right angles to OA in a point which is the harmonic conjugate of A' with respect to the circle.*

Let a chord drawn through A' cut the circle in P and P' and AL drawn at right angles to OA in Q. From O the centre of the circle draw ON bisecting PP' at N.

First consider the case in which A' is outside the circle   Let AL cut the circle at T. Then the triangles $A'AT$, $A'OT$ are similar and therefore $A'A \cdot A'O = A'T^2 = A'P \cdot A'P'$. But since the angles at A and N are right angles $AQNO$ is a cyclic quadrilateral and therefore $A'A . A'O = A'Q . A'N$.

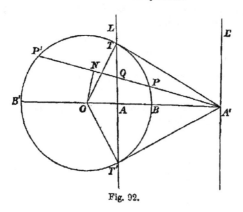

Fig. 92.

Hence

$$A'P . A'P' = A'Q . A'N = A'Q \tfrac{1}{2}(A'P + A'P').$$

Therefore
$$\frac{2}{A'Q} = \frac{1}{A'P} + \frac{1}{A'P'},$$

or $(A'PQP')$ is a harmonic range.

If A' is within the circle let $A'L$ at right angles to OA' meet the circle in T'. Then $ONAQ$ is a cyclic quadrilateral and
$$P'A' . A'P = A'T'^2 = OA' . A'A = NA' . A'Q = \tfrac{1}{2}(P'A' - A'P) A'Q.$$

Therefore

$$\frac{2}{A'Q} = \frac{1}{A'P} - \frac{1}{P'A'}, \text{ or } \frac{2}{A'Q} = \frac{1}{A'P} + \frac{1}{A'P'},$$

and therefore the range $(P'A'PQ)$ is harmonic.

Since AL divides any chord drawn through A' harmonically with respect to the circle it is the polar of A'. Hence *the polar of any point with respect to a circle passes through the inverse point and is at right angles to the radius upon which the points lie.*

101. *If A lies upon the polar of B, then B lies upon the polar of A.*

Let A' and B' be the points inverse to A and B respectively with respect to the circle. Then since $OA . OA' = OB . OB'$, $AA'BB'$ is a cyclic quadrilateral. But $AB'B$ is a right angle

9—2

since A lies upon the polar of B. Hence $AA'B$ is also a right angle and therefore B lies upon the polar of A.

Two points A and B such that each lies upon the polar of the other are called *conjugate*.

If we call the polar of A, a; and the polar of B, b, the above theorem may be enunciated thus :—

If a passes through the pole of b then b passes through the pole of a.

Two lines a and b such that each contains the pole of the other are called *conjugate*.

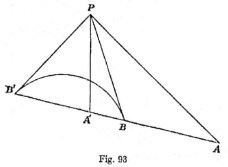

Fig. 93

If A and A' are a pair of conjugate points, and if the line AA' cuts the circle in BB', then the range $(ABA'B')$ is harmonic, since A' lies upon the polar of A. Let the tangents at B and B' meet at P. Then P is the pole of BB', and it therefore lies both upon the polar of A and upon the polar of A'. PA and PA' are conjugate lines and the pencil $P(ABA'B')$ is harmonic. Hence any two conjugate lines and the tangents from their point of intersection form a harmonic pencil.

If A and B are conjugate points, and C is the intersection of the polars of A and B, then C is conjugate both to A and to B. ABC forms a triangle such that each angular point is the pole of the opposite side and is called a *self-conjugate* triangle.

Special cases of the above theorems arise when we consider a pole at the centre or at infinity. The centre of the circle is the pole of the line at infinity. Conversely the polar of a point at infinity passes through the centre, in other words diameters are the polars of points at infinity.

A line conjugate to a diameter is at right angles to the diameter, and in particular, conjugate diameters are at right angles to one another.

Hence a self-conjugate triangle, one of whose angular points is the centre of the circle, must be right-angled and have the line at infinity as one side.

102. Properties of a quadrangle inscribed in a circle.

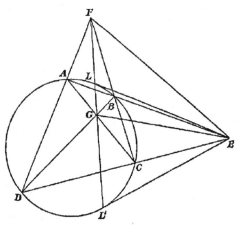

Fig. 94.

Let $ABCD$ be the inscribed quadrangle. Let AB, CD meet at E; DA, CB at F; and DB, CA at G. Join EF, FG, GE.

Then the pencil $F(AGBE)$ is harmonic, and therefore FE and FG are conjugate lines with respect to the circle. Similarly EF and EG are conjugate, and likewise GE and GF. Hence EFG is a self-conjugate triangle.

Since FG and FE are conjugate lines, FG is the polar of E, and therefore if FG cut the circle in L and L', EL and EL' are the tangents from E to the circle.

We have therefore the following construction for the polar of any point E. Draw any two chords EBA, ECD. Let CD, DA meet at F; CA, BD at G. Then FG is the line required.

If E is without the circle the polar cuts the circle in the points of contact of the tangents from E.

If it be required to find the pole of a given line, we can find in the above manner the polars of any two points upon it, and their intersection is the point required.

103 *Any number of points on a line form a range homographic with the pencil formed by their polars.*

Let the points be $A, B, C, \ldots$ upon the line s, and let their polars be $a, b, c, \ldots$ meeting at S the pole of s. Then if O is the centre of the circle, $a, b, c, \ldots$ are respectively perpendicular to $OA, OB, OC, \ldots$. Hence

$$\{ABC\ldots\} = O\{ABC\ldots\} = \{abc\ldots\}.$$

104 *Pairs of conjugate points upon a line form a range in involution.*

Let the pairs of points be A, A'; B, B'; C, C'; $\ldots$ upon the line s. Let their polars be a, a'; b, b'; c, c'; $\ldots$ meeting at S the pole of s. Then a' is SA, a is SA', and so on. By the previous theorem

$$\{AA', BB', CC'\} = \{aa', bb', cc'\} = S\{A'A, B'B, C'C\}$$
$$= \{A'A, B'B, C'C\}.$$

Hence the range is in involution.

The double points of the involution are the points where the line cuts the circle.

Pairs of conjugate lines through a point form a pencil in involution.

Let the lines be a, a'; b, b'; c, c'; $\ldots$ through the point S, and let their poles be A, A': B, B'; C, C'; $\ldots$ upon the line s. Then $\{aa', bb', cc'\} = \{AA', BB', CC'\} = S\{AA', BB', CC'\} = \{a'a, b'b, c'c\}$. Hence the pencil is in involution.

The double lines of the involution are the tangents from S to the circle.

105 *Any line cuts a circle and the opposite sides of a quadrangle inscribed in the circle in pairs of points in involution.*

Let $ABCD$ be the quadrangle and let the line cut the circle in PP', and AB, CD, BC, DA, AC, BD in Q, Q', R, R', S, S' respectively.

Then

$$\{PP'R'Q\} = A\,\{PP'DB\} = C\,\{PP'DB\} = \{PP'Q'R$$

Hence $\{PP'R'Q\} = \{P'PRQ'\}$ and therefore $(PP',\,QQ',\,RR')$ are in involution.

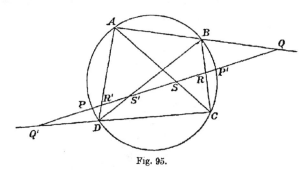

Fig. 95.

If D coincides with A, AD becomes the tangent at A. Hence *if a line cuts a circle in PP', the sides BC, CA, AB of an inscribed triangle in R, Q', Q and the tangent at A in R', then $(PP',\,QQ',\,RR')$ are in involution.*

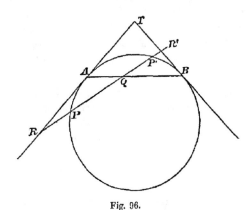

Fig. 96.

If D coincides with A, and C with B, AD and BC become a pair of tangents TA, TB touching the circle at A and B. S then coincides with S', and Q and Q', and is therefore a double point of the involution.

Hence *if a line cuts a circle in PP', two tangents in RR', and the chord of contact in Q, Q is a double point of the involution determined by PP', RR'.*

106. *The pair of tangents drawn from any point to a circle and the pairs of lines drawn from the same point to opposite vertices of a quadrilateral circumscribing a circle form pairs of lines in involution.*

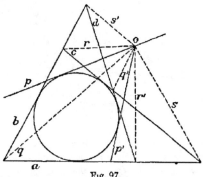

Fig. 97.

Let a, b, c, d be the sides of the quadrilateral, let the tangents from the given point O be pp', and let the lines drawn from O to the intersections of ab, cd, bc, da, ac, bd, be q, q', r, r', s, s' respectively.

Then $\{pp'r'q\} = a\{pp'db\} = c\{pp'db\} = \{pp'q'r\}$.

Hence $\{pp'r'q\} = \{p'prq'\}$ and therefore (pp', qq', rr') are in involution.

If d coincides with a, ad becomes the point of contact of the tangent a. Hence *if from a point O tangents pp' are drawn to a circle, lines r, q', q to the angular points bc, ca, ab of a circumscribing triangle and r' to the point of contact of a, then (pp', qq', rr') are in involution.*

If d coincides with a, and c with b, ad and bc become the points of contact of the tangents a and b. Then s coincides with s', and q and q', and is therefore a double ray of the involution.

Hence *if from a point O tangents pp' are drawn to a circle, lines rr' to two points on the circle and q to the point of intersection of the tangents at these points, q is a double ray of the involution determined by pp', rr'.*

107. Harmonic and involution properties of a conic. All the theorems which have been proved for ranges and pencils related to a circle which are harmonic or in involution remain valid when the circle is projected into a conic.

Thus a point and its polar regarded as the locus of the point conjugate with regard to the given point on any chord drawn through the latter project into a point and line bearing the same relation to one another with respect to the conic. If the point be outside the conic, its polar is the chord of contact of the tangents from the point. If the point lies on the conic its polar is the tangent at the point.

Conjugate points and lines project into conjugate points and lines with respect to the conic.

Self-conjugate triangles project into self-conjugate triangles.

The properties of an inscribed quadrangle are true for the conic; and the constructions for the polar of a point and for the tangents from any point also apply to the conic.

108. Centre of a conic.

The *centre* of a conic is the *pole of the line at infinity*. The line at infinity in the plane of the conic is in general the projection of a line at a finite distance in the plane of the circle of which the conic is the projection, and the centre of the circle is not the pole of a line at a finite distance. Hence the centre of the conic is not in general the projection of the centre of the circle. This is the case, however, when the projection is orthogonal.

The centre of a parabola is at infinity, for the line at infinity is the projection of a tangent to the circle of which the parabola is the projection, and the pole of a tangent is its point of contact. Hence in this case the pole is also projected to infinity.

The centre of a conic bisects every chord through it. Let the chord PP' pass through the centre C, and let C' be the point at infinity on the chord. Then the range $\{PCP'C'\}$ is harmonic, and since C' is at infinity $PC = CP'$. Hence a conic is symmetrical with respect to the centre.

109. Diameters of a conic. A diameter of a conic is a chord through the centre.

Since the centre of a parabola is at infinity all its diameters are parallel.

Let PCP' be any diameter of a conic and QNQ' a chord conjugate to the diameter meeting it at N. Then the pole of PCP' lies upon QNQ' at infinity, and since N is the harmonic conjugate of the pole it bisects QQ'.

Since all chords conjugate to PCP' pass through the pole of PCP' at infinity they are parallel, and hence we obtain the theorem:—A diameter is the locus of the middle points of the system of parallel chords to which it is conjugate. Of these chords one is a diameter, and it will in like manner bisect chords parallel to the first diameter. Hence *each of two conjugate diameters bisects chords parallel to the other*.

Conjugate diameters form a pencil in involution. But a pencil in involution always contains one pair of rays at right angles to one another, and therefore there will always be a pair of conjugate diameters at right angles to one another. (Arts. 96, 104.)

The *axes of a conic* are the conjugate diameters at right angles.

The axis of a parabola is the diameter which is at right angles to the chords conjugate to it.

110. Asymptotes of a conic. The asymptotes of a conic are the tangents from the centre; their chord of contact is the line at infinity. They are clearly real only in the case of the hyperbola.

Since the tangents from any point to a conic are harmonically conjugate with respect to any pair of conjugate lines drawn through the point, it follows that the asymptotes and any pair of conjugate diameters form a harmonic pencil.

The asymptotes are therefore the double lines of the pencil in involution formed by the system of conjugate diameters.

VI. Problems of the Second Degree.

Problems which involve in their solution the determination of the common points or rays of homographic ranges or pencils are said to be of the second degree. Algebraically they are equivalent to the solution of a quadratic equation

111. *Given five points S_1, S_2, A, B, C on a conic, to determine the points of intersection of the curve with a given straight line p.*

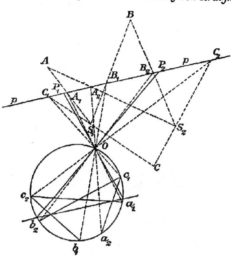

Fig. 98.

If S_1, S_2 be joined to each of the points A, B, C, the pencils $S_1(A, B, C, ...)$ and $S_2(A, B, C, ...)$ will be homographic and will form two homographic ranges $(A_1, B_1, C_1, ...)$ and $(A_2, B_2, C_2, ...)$ upon the line p. The common points P_1 and P_2 of these ranges will be points on the conic, since pairs of corresponding rays of the pencils will meet in P_1 and P_2. Hence P_1 and P_2 are the required points of intersection. The common points are found by the construction in Art. 78.

112. *Given five tangents s_1, s_2, a, b, c to a conic, to determine the tangents to the conic from a given point P.* (Fig. 99.)

If s_1, s_2 intersect each of the other tangents in the points A_1, B_1, C_1 ... and A_2, B_2, C_2 ... respectively, these points will form two homographic ranges, and if they be joined to P we obtain two homographic pencils $P(A_1, B_1, C_1, ...)$ and $P(A_2, B_2, C_2, ...)$. The common rays t_1, t_2 of these pencils will be tangents to the conic.

113. Particular cases of the two preceding constructions.

1. *To find the directions of the asymptotes of a conic through five points.*

In Art. 111 suppose the line p to be the line at infinity. Lines drawn from any finite point to P_1 and P_2 are parallel to the asymptotes.

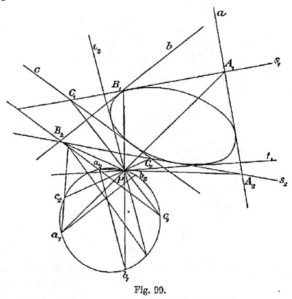

Fig. 99.

If O is the vertex of the homographic pencils

$$O\,(A_1B_1C_1\ldots),\ \ O\,(A_2B_2C_2\ldots)$$

the rays $OA_1,\ OA_2,\ OB_1,\ OB_2\ldots$ are parallel to $S_1A_1,\ S_2A_2,\ S_1B_1,\ S_2B_2\ldots$ respectively.

2. *Given five points on a conic, to construct the tangents from any point to the conic.*

Determine by Pascal's theorem the tangents at each of the five points and then make use of the construction in Art. 112

3. *Given five tangents to a conic, to find the points in which any line cuts the conic.*

Determine by Brianchon's theorem the points of contact of the tangents and then make use of the construction in Art. 111.

4. *Given four tangents to a parabola, draw the tangents from a given point.*

The fifth tangent is the line at infinity.

5. *Given four tangents to a parabola, find the points of intersection with a given line.*

6. *Given the asymptotes and a point on a conic draw the tangents from a given point.*

114 *Given five points on a conic, to find the centre, the axes and the asymptotes.*

Let A, B, C, D, E be the five given points. Through A draw a line AX parallel to BC, and find the point A' in which AX again meets the conic. Let AC and BA' meet at K, and AB and CA' at L. Then KL bisects both AA' and BC and is the diameter conjugate to these chords. In the same manner determine the diameter MN which bisects DE or any other chord. The centre O will be the point of intersection of KL and MN.

If KL is parallel to MN, O is at infinity and the conic is a parabola. KL and MN are parallel to the axis of the parabola.

Having determined two diameters OK and OM, through O draw OK' parallel to BC and OM' parallel to DE. Then OK and OK' are conjugate diameters, so also are OM and OM'. These two pairs of conjugate diameters determine an involution of which the double rays are the asymptotes, and the pair of rays at right angles the axes.

The points in which the axes cut the conic can be determined in the usual manner and thus their lengths found.

115. *Given four points $ABCD$ and a line t, to construct a conic passing through the points and touching the line.*

We have first to determine the point of contact of the tangent t, and then five points being known the conic may be constructed in the usual manner.

If any conic be described through $ABCD$ it will cut the line t in points which form an involution with the points where t cuts the opposite sides of the quadrangle $ABCD$, and therefore if t touches the conic the point of contact will be a double point of the involution.

Let t cut AB, CD, BC, DA in Q, Q', R, R' respectively, and let P_1, P_2 be the double points of the involution determined by Q, Q', R, R'. Then either of the conics $ABCDP_1$ or $ABCDP_2$ is a solution of the problem.

If there are no double points no conic can be described satisfying the conditions.

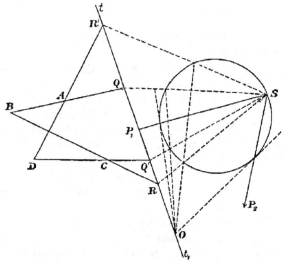

Fig. 100.

116   *Given four lines a, b, c, d and a point T to construct a conic touching the lines and passing through the point.*

Determine the double rays of the pencil in involution formed by lines drawn from T to opposite intersections of the sides of the quadrilateral a, b, c, d. Either of the double rays will be a tangent to the required conic; and hence five tangents being known the conic can be described. There will be two conics, one corresponding to each double ray.

If there are no double rays no conic can be described satisfying the conditions.

117.   Particular cases of the two preceding constructions.

1.   *To construct a parabola passing through four given points.*

Let A, B, C, D be the four points, the conic through them has to touch the line at infinity. Hence we have to determine the double points of the involution which the line at infinity makes with the sides of the quadrangle $ABCD$. To do this take any point O, and from it draw rays q, q', r, r' parallel to AB, CD, AC, BD respectively. The double rays pp' of the involution determined by q, q', r, r' meet the line at infinity in the double points of the involution. Hence the double rays are parallel to the axes of the two parabolas which can be described. See Art. 90.

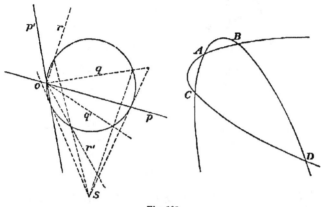

Fig. 101.

2. *Construct a parabola touching three given lines and passing through a given point.*

118 *Given three points A, B, C and two lines t_1 and t_2, to describe a conic passing through the points and touching the lines.*

We have first to determine the points of contact of the given lines with the conic; then five points being known, the conic can be described.

Let AB meet t_1 and t_2 in C_1 and C_2, and let AC meet t_1 and t_2 in B_1 and B_2. Let Z_1, Z_2 be the double points of the involution determined by (AB, C_1C_2) and Y_1Y_2 the double points of the involution determined by (AC, B_1B_2). Take any one of the four lines Z_1Y_1, Z_1Y_2, Z_2Y_1, Z_2Y_2 and let it meet t_1 and t_2 in P_1 and P_2. Then a conic through $ABCP_1P_2$ will touch t_1 and t_2.

For, by the theorem of Art. 105, if a conic is described touching the lines at P_1P_2 and passing through A, it must cut AB in the point conjugate to A in the involution of which Z_1 is a double point and C_1 and C_2 conjugate points. Hence it passes through B the point conjugate to A. There are four solutions of the problem.

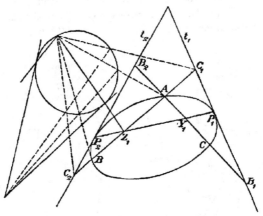

Fig. 102.

119. *Given three lines a, b, c and two points T_1 and T_2 to describe a conic touching the lines and passing through the points.*

Let c_1, c_2 be the lines joining T_1 and T_2 to the intersection of a, b, and let b_1, b_2 be the lines joining T_1 and T_2 to the intersection of a, c. Let $z_1 z_2$ be the double rays of the involution determined by $(ab, c_1 c_2)$ and $y_1 y_2$ the double rays of the involution determined by $(ac, b_1 b_2)$. Take any one of the four points of intersection of y_1 and y_2 with z_1 and z_2, and let p_1 and p_2 be the lines joining this point to T_1 and T_2. Then p_1 and p_2 will be tangents to the conic. Since five tangents are known the conic can be constructed.

MISCELLANEOUS CONSTRUCTIONS AND EXAMPLES.

120 *Given five points $ABCDE$ of a conic, to construct the polar of a given point S*

Join SA and SB and by Pascal's theorem determine the points A' and B' in which these lines again cut the conic. Let AB, $A'B'$ meet at K and AB', $A'B$ at L. Then LK is the polar of S.

Given five points $ABCDE$ of a conic, to construct the pole of a given line s.

Take any two points upon s and find their polars by the preceding construction. The point of intersection of the polars will be the pole of s. For simplicity it is convenient to take the two points on S to be the points of intersection of AB and CD with the line.

1. *Given five tangents to a conic construct the pole of a given line.*

2. *Given five tangents to a conic construct the polar of a given point.*

121. *Given four tangents to a conic and the point of contact of one of them to construct the conic.*

Let the tangents be a, b, s_1, s_2 and let the point of contact of s_1 be given. We may then regard s_1 as a double tangent, a fifth tangent c coinciding with it so that the limiting position of the point of intersection s_1c is the point of contact of s.

Proceed as in the general case (Art. 81), taking P_1, P_2 upon a. The line joining the point of contact of s_1 to P_1 is c_1, and c_2 is the line joining P_2 to the intersection of s_1s_2. Also b_1 and b_2 are the lines joining P_1 and P_2 to the intersections of s_1, b and s_2, b respectively. Let p be the line joining the intersections of c_1, c_2 and b_1, b_2, then any number of tangents may be found by taking points upon p. Let one of these points be D, and let d_1 and d_2 be the lines joining it to P_1 and P_2. Then the line joining the intersections of s_1, d_1 and s_2, d_2 is a tangent.

1. *Given four tangents to a parabola construct the curve.*

2. *Given three tangents to a parabola and the point of contact of one of them construct the curve.*

3. *Given three tangents to a conic and the points of contact of two of them construct the curve.*

4. *Given three tangents and an asymptote construct the conic.*

5. *Given a tangent and two asymptotes construct the conic.*

ADDITIONAL EXAMPLES.

1. *Given two right lines, OA and O'B, Fig. 103, which do not, when produced, meet on the paper, to draw through a given point, P, a right line which passes through their point of intersection.*

Through *P* draw any line meeting *OA* and *O'B* in *m* and *n*; draw any line, *rs*, parallel to *mn*, meeting the given lines in *r* and *s*; divide *rs*, at *Q*, into segments *rQ*, *sQ* proportional to *mP* and *nP*; then *PQ* will, if produced, pass through the point of intersection of *OA* and *O'B*.

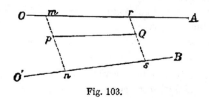

Fig. 103.

2. *Through three given points, A, B, C, Fig. 104, to draw a circle when the centre of the circle is off the paper.*

Draw lines *AB*, *BC*; bisect them in *m* and *n*, and at *m*, *n* draw perpendiculars, *mp*, *nq*, to *AB*, *BC*; then *mp* and *nq* meet in the centre of the required circle. Through *B* draw (by the last example) a line, *Br*, passing through the point of intersection

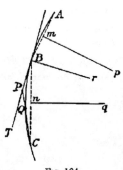

Fig. 104.

of mp and nq; at B draw BT perpendicular to Br; then BT is a tangent to the required circle at B. Take any point, P, on BT; draw PC, and on PC take Q such that $PC . PQ = PB^2$; then Q is a point on the circle; and thus, by varying P, any number of points on the circular arc can be found.

3. *Given the curve $y = f(x)$, construct the curve $y = \dfrac{f(x)}{x^2 + n^2}$, where n is a given quantity.*

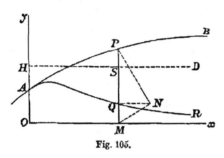

Fig. 105.

We may suppose that y, x, and n are numbers, or that they are linear quantities. If the latter, the equation to be represented will be given in the form $y = \dfrac{k^2}{x^2 + n^2} \cdot f(x)$, where k is a given linear quantity, and of course $f(x)$ will also be a linear quantity.

Let us suppose that y, x, n are numerical for simplicity, and let APB be the curve $y = f(x)$. Take OH, on the axis of y, equal to n, and draw HD parallel to Ox. Let PM be any value of y, and let it meet HD in S; then

$$OM = x = SM \tan OSM = n \tan OSM = n \tan \phi,$$

suppose. Hence, if y' is the ordinate of the required curve,

$$y' = \frac{y}{n^2 \sec^2 \phi} = \frac{1}{n^2} \cdot y \cos^2 \phi.$$

Draw MN parallel to OS; let fall PN perpendicular to MN, and draw NQ perpendicular to PM.

Then $MN = y \cos \phi$, and $MQ = MN \cos \phi = y \cos^2 \phi$. Hence

$$y' = \frac{1}{n^2} \cdot QM.$$

Giving P various positions along the curve APB, we have the curve AQR which is the locus of Q; and we see that the required curve, $y = \dfrac{f(x)}{x^2 + n^2}$, is obtained by multiplying all the ordinates of AQR by the constant $\dfrac{1}{n^2}$.

4. *A and B are two fixed points 8 cms. apart; if r, r' are the distances of a point P from A and B, respectively, represent all values of r, r' which satisfy the equation*

$$3r^2 - 5r'^2 = 30 \quad \ldots\ldots\ldots\ldots\ldots\ldots\ldots(1).$$

It is well known that the locus of a point whose distances from A and B satisfy the equation $lr^2 + mr'^2 = k$ is a circle whose centre lies on AB at the point, C, which divides AB so that $\dfrac{AC}{CB} = \dfrac{m}{l}$, and the square of the radius

$$= \frac{1}{l+m}\left[k - \frac{lm}{(l+m)^2} AB^2\right].$$

If l and m have opposite signs, the point C lies on AB or BA produced.

In the case above, C lies beyond B at a distance of 12 cms., and the radius of the circle is 15.

Another way of representing the values of r and r' is to adopt the method of Art. 30.   Let $r^2 = x$, $r'^2 = y$, where x, y are the rectangular co-ordinates of a point; construct, then, the right line whose equation is $3x - 5y = 30$, and take the positive values of x and y; the square roots of such values are the distances of P from A and B; but the range of points on the line is limited by the consideration that the sum $\sqrt{x} + \sqrt{y}$ must be > 8; and $\sqrt{x} - \sqrt{y}$ must be < 8.

5. *Solve the equation* $7 \cos 2\theta = 4 \sin\theta - 3 \cos\theta$

The right-hand side is $5 \sin(\theta - 36° 54')$.   See Art. 33.

Result: $\theta = 154° 39' 30''$.

6. *Show that the equation*

$$e^{\frac{x}{5}} + e^{-\frac{x}{5}} = 6 \sin\frac{2x - 45}{40}$$

has no real solutions.

7. *Solve the equation*

$$e^{\frac{x}{5}} + e^{-\frac{x}{5}} = 6 \sin \frac{2x + 45}{40}.$$

Result: $x = 8{\cdot}8$ and $x = -6{\cdot}9$.

8. *Solve the equation* $3 \sin x = 2x + 3$.

Result: $x = -2{\cdot}453$.

9. *Solve the equation* $4 \sin \dfrac{2x - 5}{3} = 5 - x$.

(Let $z = \dfrac{2x - 5}{3}$. Result: $z = {\cdot}467$, $x = 3{\cdot}2$.)

10. *Solve the equation* $4 \cos \dfrac{2x - 5}{3} = 5 - x$.

Result: $x = 1{\cdot}639$; $4{\cdot}769$; $8{\cdot}189$.

[Let $\dfrac{2x - 5}{3} = z$; then $\cos z = \dfrac{5 - 3z}{8}$. If we have a curve of sines such as $OVUE$, Art. 22, we have merely to take as the axis from which z is reckoned that through V perpendicular to OE, and the curve serves as a curve of cosines.]

11. *Given the quantities* a, b, c, m, n, *solve the equation*

$$m \log (x - a) + n \log (x - c) = (m + n) \log (x - b).$$

[This is $\qquad \left(\dfrac{x - a}{x - b}\right)^{m} = \left(\dfrac{x - b}{x - c}\right)^{n}$.

Let $x - a = \lambda (x - b)$, and $x - c = \mu (x - b)$, where λ and μ are to be found. Then we have

$$\lambda^{m} \mu^{n} = 1, \text{ and } (b - c) \lambda + (a - b) \mu = a - c.$$

Take two rectangular axes of λ and μ, and construct the curve $\lambda^{m} \mu^{n} = 1$, and the right line denoted by the second equation. Both pass through the point $(1, 1)$, and have another point of intersection.]

12. *Show that the dipolar angles* θ, ϕ *which satisfy the equation* $m \sin \theta + n \sin \phi = k$ *can be represented thus:*

With any points A and B as centres describe circles of radii m and n, respectively; draw a right line HK parallel to AB and at a distance k from it; take any point, M, on the first circle, and let MQ be the perpendicular from M on HK; on the second circle let N be a point whose perpendicular distance from AB is equal to MQ; then the lines AM and BN intersect in a point P such that $PAB = \theta$, $PBA = \phi$.   (See also p. 55.)

13   *Represent as dipolar angles all values of* θ, ϕ *which satisfy*
$$m \cos \theta = n \cos \phi.$$

Write it $n \sec \theta = m \sec \phi$; draw a line AO equal to n, and produce it through O to B so that $OB = m$; at O draw Oy perpendicular to AB; let R be any point on Oy; inflect BS equal to AR, S being on Oy; then AR and BS meet in a point P such that $PAB = \theta$, $PBA = \phi$.

14. *Solve the equation* $(a + b \sin^2 \theta) \cos \theta = k$.

Construct the curves whose polar equations are $r = \dfrac{k}{\cos \theta}$ and $r = a + b \sin^2 \theta$. The first is a right line; the second is constructed thus: write its equation $r = a + \dfrac{b}{2} - \dfrac{b}{2} \cos 2\theta$; take $OA = b$ and on OA as diameter describe a circle, whose centre is C; on CA as diameter describe a circle; round C as centre describe a circle of radius $a + \dfrac{b}{2}$; let P be a point on the first circle, and POA a value of θ; let PC meet the second circle in Q; then $QCA = 2\theta$, $CQ = \dfrac{b}{2} \cos 2\theta$; if CQ meets the third circle in R, $QR = a + \dfrac{b}{2} - \dfrac{b}{2} \cos 2\theta$; on OP take a point X so that $OX = QR$; then the locus of X is the curve $r = a + b \sin^2 \theta$.

Another way of constructing this curve is this: draw OA, from which θ is measured; at O draw OB perpendicular to OA; round O as centre describe a circle of radius b; let P be any point on this circle, $POA = \theta$; drop PQ perpendicular to OB; from Q draw QR perpendicular to OP; then $OR = b \sin^2 \theta$; on OP produced take S such that $RS = a$; then the locus of S is the curve.

The first method is preferable because the second requires the drawing of two perpendiculars.

In the second way we can also draw the curve $r = a + b \sin^n \theta$.

15   *Draw the curves* $r \cos \theta = a$, $r \cos^3 \theta = a$, ... $r \cos^{2n+1} \theta = a$.

For example, take the locus $r \cos^3 \theta = a$. Diaw $OA = a$; at A erect AB perpendicular to OA; let P be any point on OB; draw OP; at P draw PQ perpendicular to OP, meeting OA in Q; at Q draw QR perpendicular to OQ, meeting OP in R. The locus of R, as P is varied, is the curve $r \cos^3 \theta = a$. Similarly for $r \cos^{2n+1} \theta = a$.

16   *Draw the curves* $r \cos^2 \theta = a$, $r \cos^4 \theta = a$, ... $r \cos^{2n} \theta = a$.

Draw OA, from which θ is measured; about O describe a circle of radius a; let P be any point on this circle; at P draw PQ perpendicular to OP, meeting OA in Q; at Q draw QR perpendicular to OQ, meeting OP in R; the locus of R, as P varies, is the curve required. Similarly for $r \cos^{2n} \theta = a$.

17.   *Draw the curve* $y = \tan x$.

See Figs. 21, 22 of Art. 22. Draw the circle ABA' of radius unity; draw OE equal to the circumference, at A draw the tangent to the circle; produce the lines $C1$, $C2$, $C3$, ... to meet this tangent in the points $p_1, p_2, p_3, ...$; from these points draw parallels to OE meeting the ordinates at

$$n_1, n_2, n_3, ... \text{ in } P_1, P_2, P_3, ...;$$

these latter points determine the curve.

18.   *Draw the curve* $y = a \tan \dfrac{x - c}{b}$.

Same process; see Figs. 24, 25.

Similarly draw the curve $y = a \sec \dfrac{x - c}{b}$.

19.   *Hence find the solutions of* $a \tan \dfrac{x - c}{b} = f(x)$, *where* $f(x)$ *is any given function of* x.

20.   *Solve the equation* $(a + b \sin^2 \theta) \cos^2 \theta = k$.

21.   *The values of the constants* c, b, n *in the equation*

$$v = \frac{c}{(1 + bt)^n}$$

being unknown, show how to find them graphically when we know three values of v *corresponding to three values of* t. (Slotte's equation for the viscosity of water.)

Combine a right line with a curve of the form $y = x^m$, where m is given. (See Ex. 11.)

CAMBRIDGE : PRINTED BY JOHN CLAY, M.A. AT THE UNIVERSITY PRESS.

CPSIA information can be obtained
at www.ICGtesting.com
Printed in the USA
BVHW041918130619
550959BV00007B/29/P